Essays in Gratitude

ESSAYS IN GRATITUDE

D. ELTON TRUEBLOOD

BROADMAN PRESS
Nashville, Tennessee

4269-38

ISBN: 0-8054-6938-9

Dewey Decimal Classification: 814

Library of Congress Catalog Card Number: 82-071215

Printed in the United States of America

Contents

Preface

When, in 1974, Harper & Row published my autobiography, *While It Is Day*, my wife teased me, saying that the book was only volume 1. She was partly right! She understood, of course, that the declared intention to write no more books did not preclude the issuing of collections of separate writings previously printed. Four of these have actually appeared, and now it seems right to edit a fifth collection, produced in a different fashion.

The separate essays in this volume have already appeared, on a monthly schedule, in the magazine *Quaker Life*, the editor, Jack Kirk, now graciously permitting their republication in book form. The present collection has come to pass primarily because of the encouragement of Johnnie Godwin of Broadman Press. The essays, which are now bound together for the first time, have a theme in common, that of personal gratitude. That is the reason for the title.

Though this volume is frankly personal, it is not really an autobiography, since it is not primarily about the author. Instead, it is about other people, very many people. That is why the new volume contains so many names and has an index. Being akin to autobiography, and certainly a supplement to the one already issued, this book necessarily employs the first person singular pronoun, even though I wish that it could be avoided, and though it has been my normal practice, in most of my writings, to avoid it. While the use of this pronoun is unavoidable, the reader will soon notice that the chief emphasis is upon others, particularly others to whom I am consciously indebted. Because there are so many who have helped at every turn of the way, my sense of personal obligation is one of the major elements of my recollections. What I cannot repay I can at least acknowledge, and this volume is one practical means of accomplishing such a purpose. The brevity of the essays is intentional. I am writing for busy people who prefer the lean style.

It is strange that the phrase "a self-made man" should ever have gained general acceptance, since no such creature exists. Each human being is constantly being made and remade, by outside influences, most of which are personal. It is some recognition of this important fact that has led me, in my eighty-second year, to undertake the toil of issuing yet another book. Wordsworth wrote *The Prelude* to report the "Growth of a Poet's Mind," and now it may be the duty of one who does not claim to be a poet to describe some of the personal forces which have enabled his mind to grow. With this purpose in mind, I send forth another volume. I send it forth with as much joy as I felt when I dispatched the first production of my faithful pen. As I do so, I include my readers in the pattern of conscious indebtedness, for, if there were no readers, writing would be a largely worthless enterprise.

D. ELTON TRUEBLOOD

Earlham
Winter, 1982

I
The Blessings of Maturity

Old age is easy for me to bear, and it is not
only not painful, but positively a joy.

Cicero

In Plato's *Republic*, we are told of a conversation which occurred between Socrates and Cephalus, in which Socrates is reported as saying, "There is nothing which for my part I like better, Cephalus, than conversing with aged men; for I regard them as travelers who have gone on a journey which I too may have to go, and of whom I ought to inquire whether the way is smooth and easy, or rugged and difficult . . . Is life harder towards the end?" The essence of the old man's reply was that "old age has a great sense of calm and freedom."

Being now older than Socrates was when he died, I am in a position similar to that of the old man in the greatest of Plato's works. Like him, I am pleased to be able to share anything which I have been able to learn on life's journey, by telling what I can about the condition of the road which we are all destined to travel.

Never ignoring or denying the physical hardships of old age, I nevertheless affirm that the joys of my maturity have been very great indeed. The calmness and freedom of which Cephalus spoke are real! The fact that autumn is, in many ways, the most beautiful season of the year is a parable of human life, as well as a fact of nature. The slower pace is itself a remarkable blessing. I rejoice each morning, as I face the day, that, in contrast to all of my former life, I do not have more insistent responsibilities than I am able to accomplish. If I wish to do so, I can just sit and be grateful. Fortunately, I can do this without infringing upon some duty which is necessary, either for my own survival or for the welfare of others.

It came to me as something of a surprise to discover that the last chapter of life could be so enjoyable. Of course, I should not have been surprised, for I had been told; but we tend to be slow of understanding. That wise man, Dr. Samuel Johnson, made the point unmistakenly when he said that "vernal flowers, however beautiful and gay, are only intended by nature as preparatives to autumn fruits." It has amazed me to realize that these profound words were written by the famous sage when he was only forty years old. I have now lived longer than did the scholar from whom I have gladly learned for many years, and this I recognize as an unearned blessing.

We may wish that Dr. Johnson had been allowed more years in which to enjoy the fruits of a life so strenuously spent, but perhaps it was better that he should die when he did. At least he was relieved of some excruciating pain. It is moving to us to remember that, at the end, the brave man refused to take any more sedatives for the alleviation of his agony. When told by his attending physician that he could not recover without a miracle, Johnson replied, "Then I will take no more physic, not even opiates; for I have prayed that I may render my soul to God unclouded."

I am certainly grateful for the fact that I have lived as long as I have, partly because the time allotted to me permits me to assemble my memories in some semblance of order. The outcome is that time never seems to drag. Each added day affords me an opportunity to remember some event or some person, already partly forgotten, but now recovered with vividness. This is what we mean by the gathering of the autumn fruits without the sense of urgency which was inevitable when the plants, destined to produce fruits, were being watered, nurtured, and tended. The more I contemplate, the more accurate the agricultural figure seems to be; in a sense I have been a farmer all of my life.

In thinking what Plato intended by stressing the freedom which old age may provide, I begin to understand. In what sense am I more free than I was in earlier years? Part of my freedom is freedom from hurry. Of course I have not totally abandoned travel, and am, as I write these words, planning another trip to England; but my good fortune is that I can now make my plans without being hectic. Because I am not trying to do too much, I can savor each step of the journey.

It would be ridiculous for me to claim that I shall give no more public addresses because I cannot now know what are the particular opportunities that will arise, but I *can* affirm that my addresses will be comparatively few. I shall not travel long distances to speak, except under circumstances which give reasonable promise that a real difference can be made. Realizing the limits of my energy, I propose to use what remains as wisely as possible and, in any case, not to waste it. The upshot is that I mean to stay home as much as I can, to tend my garden, to nurture my flowers, and to enjoy leisured thinking. Sitting in the corner of my bedroom, with the volumes of Addison and Johnson at arm's reach, seems to me so delightful that it would be foolish of me to give up such an opportunity except for some adequate reason. I may travel a little, but I shall go by train when I can arrange to do so; and, if I fly, I shall try to avoid close connections. Running through an airport to catch a departing plane seems to me a foolish act, especially for a person more than eighty years of age.

At home, there are books to be reread, and other books to be read for the first time. Here they are in my library, waiting patiently for my attention; and now, at last, I have the time. I realize that we tend to read the great books too early, before we have enough experience to understand them, and sometimes we never open them again. Such neglect is a serious mistake, which may be corrected if we continue to live. In my own case I have the blessing of the possession of a great many notebooks which go back to college days. By good fortune I discovered, very early, the value of using bound notebooks for separate courses. While loose leaves tend to become lost or scattered, the bound notebook can be retained intact and placed upon a shelf, like a published volume. I am glad that I bought my notebooks long ago in Harvard Square because they can be enjoyed over and over in my present life. Though the sentences remain exactly as I put them down nearly sixty years ago, the experience is improved by being renewed.

Every old person is a poet, at least in Wordsworth's sense of the term. We are poets because we can experience "emotion recollected in tranquility." The gratefully remembered experiences, far from being diminished by the lapse of time, may actually increase in value. Memories seem to be more enjoyable when they are put in order. If any person has lived even a moderately full life, the accumulation of his memories is literally inexhaustible. When I try to put my memories within the covers of a book, I soon realize that it would be possible for almost any person to fill thousands of pages. Recorded memories are therefore necessarily *selective*. Though many of our memories are pleasant, this is by no means true of all. If a person is honest with himself, he will recognize, in contemplation, various wrong turnings which he has made. Though these cannot be undone, they can be faced without evasion, and forgiveness can always be sought. Since not all of the fruits come to maturity in perfect condition, every person is bound to think, with Whittier, of what "might have been."

No one can write honestly about the final chapter of life without a frank facing of its problems. Not all are as fortunate as Cicero said that he was, for there are some who lose even the power to remember. Great numbers of older people suffer from arthritis and other diseases, thereby requiring constant medication, if pain is rendered endurable. I want always to recognize the problems of maturity even while I mention blessings.

Perhaps the best thing we can do is to encourage people to look upon the life of maturity without a debilitating sense of foreboding. What, unfortunately, is often demonstrated is a self-fulfilling prophecy of disaster. Though physical ailments are, of course, real, it is important to remember that attitude has a great deal to do with human well-being. Some ailments are suffered because they are expected, loss of mental power being a case in point. Though physical disabilities are sometimes inevitable, it is important to remember that there is more than one way of facing them. Here is where the dying scene of Dr. Johnson is such an antidote to despair. Though we cannot stop the pain, we can nevertheless determine, in some measure, the way in which it is encountered.

The worst evils that sometimes occur in old age are not physical, but spiritual. In some cases the older person, possibly in reaction to frustration, develops the habit of indulging in continual complaints about other people, including those who serve them most unselfishly. When this occurs it is always an occasion for sorrow because what might have been a period of peace becomes one of constant turmoil. One of the best solutions of this problem is the advance recognition of the danger, along with the conscious effort to avoid it.

Freedom from the necessity of setting everyone else straight can come at any time of life, but the conscious development of this particular freedom is especially important in declining years. It is even possible to develop the habit of deliberate silence, when pointing out the mistakes of others may do more harm than good. Though composing a letter of criticism may be therapeutic for the writer, there is no necessity of actually posting it. Instead of showing others where they are wrong, we can nurture the habit of thankfulness for what is right, being especially thankful that things are no worse than they are. In any case it helps to know that querulousness serves no useful purpose, and that, furthermore, the complaining mood is intrinsically self-defeating. When I am tempted to complain about the world situation, I find it helpful to start enumerating the things for which I have reason to be grateful.

The primary blessing of maturity is that, as Plato taught, it makes possible various forms of liberation. Many older people are liberated from the hectic struggle to get ahead in life, to build a reputation, and to establish a home. Suddenly I realize that, for the first time in my life, I do not have too many duties. Last evening I looked at my date book, in order to prepare my mind for the morning, and experienced the exquisite pleasure of observing a blank page. That does not mean that I shall do nothing today, but it does mean that whatever I do will be free from temporal pressures. I do not know, of course, what demands either the daily mail or the telephone will bring; but, right now, the space in the date book is gloriously empty. I am enjoying the clock, rather than fighting it. For many men and women in middle life this kind of freedom is never experienced. It is a particular joy of maturity to be able to produce, but to produce without strain.

The paradox of time in maturity is that we can be vividly conscious of our inevitable temporal finitude and yet enjoy its abundance, because we are in no great hurry. To know that "the night cometh" may actually be to sense a liberation from worry about lack of accomplishment, rather than the sadness which we usually associate with those sacred words. If I have only a few years in which to live, as is certainly the case, then the intelligent thing to do is to enjoy each day as though it were the last.

Another freedom of maturity is financial. For millions of people in the contemporary world, old age is the period marked by liberation from the necessity of earning. While some find it necessary to seek paid employment after the age of seventy, numbers of women and men can, because of Social Security, pensions, and personal savings, avoid entirely any search for an earned income. Even when inflation has diminished the value of savings, the older person can, in many instances, survive without financial worry, partly because the need of buying is radically reduced. In my own case, much of the freedom from financial pressure arises because I need fewer things than I once required. I am free from paying tuition, and I certainly do not need an extra car. My clothing is such that there is almost nothing in that line that I now desire. Actually I have entered a period of conscious distribution rather than of accumulation. I do not have to save for old age, for I am there already. Best of all, the freedom from earning can become liberation for service, especially, in my case, an opportunity to help people to secure proper employment, and to assist new authors in their own writing.

One of the most common misconceptions about old age is the supposition that it is always a period of intellectual decline. While, for some, decline undoubtedly occurs, this is by no means universal. When we are expressing our debt to Plato, it is good to remind ourselves that he wrote *The Laws* when he was eighty. In this magnificent final work of a brilliant mind we are far removed from the discourses which are purely Socratic, the author having achieved genuine maturity.

Many people are unaware of the numerous examples of intellectual achievements on the part of persons of advanced age and might be encouraged if told about them. Cato, the first Latin prose writer of any importance, learned Greek when he was eighty. In modern history, a brilliant example of late achievement is that of Verdi, who produced *Falstaff* on February 9, 1893, when the composer was in his eightieth year. It is a fair assumption that many persons fail to keep alert and productive because of a lack of expectancy. What is potential may be lost, not because of some physical ailment, but primarily because of lack of use. It is literally true that what we do not use, we lose.

Dr. Johnson's well-known example is a source of encouragement to many who know his story, chiefly because of Boswell's famous *Life*. Of the one hundred known prayers of Johnson, the one which has the greatest appeal for many of his loyal readers is his "Last Prayer," composed shortly before he died. With the *Dictionary*, *The Rambler*, and *The Lives of the Poets* far behind him, the reverent man had not lost his ability to create memorable phrases. In my own judgment, Johnson never created a more felicitous combination of words than when he wrote, "Make this commemoration available to the confirmation of my faith, the establishment of my hope, and the enlargement of my charity." Even to the very end, in spite of constant sickness and excruciating pain, Johnson was producing what, years earlier, he had termed "autumn fruits." Even in 1752 the brave man had already written, "To faint or loiter, when only the last efforts are required, is to steer the ship through tempests, and abandon it to the winds in sight of land; it is to break the ground and scatter the seeds and at last to neglect the harvest."

I boldly affirm that, after eighty, I can memorize either poetry or prose as rapidly as I ever could. Part of this is because I have so much uninterrupted time to devote to a valuable task. I can also affirm that the daily disciplines of prayer and Scripture grow more valuable with the added years. If I needed spiritual resources earlier, I need them even more now; and fortunately, my time for them is abundant. Part of the reason for the possibility of productivity in old age is the accumulation of resources. In this sense, I am richer than I was in any earlier period of my life. When I speak or write today, I speak and write out of the overflow.

In my own experiences, the gift of temporal freedom provides me with the opportunity of using each added day in the fashion which is most productive in my particular situation. For example, I now understand that the most productive part of any day, for me, is that from 7:30 to 9:00 AM. In this hour and a half I feel as strong as I felt in my younger years and seem to think more clearly than at any other time of my life. The intelligent procedure, then, is to guard the time and to employ it creatively. Nearly all of this particular book has been produced in this precious ninety-minute period. When my prime time is over, I often need to rest or to change my pace. A valued contemporary once helped me by saying, "I'm a pretty good man, up to eleven AM." Of course, I recognized that the remark was intended to be humorous; but, as is often the case with humor, my friend was expressing something profoundly true.

One of the blessings of maturity which is seldom sufficiently recognized is that of genuine humility. In early life there is a strong tendency to suppose that we have all of the answers, but some experience of life can cure this malady. One mark of intellectual growth is the recognition that there *are* no simple answers. The simple answers, we finally realize, are always wrong, because the world is not simple! The mystery of life, far from being dispelled by added years, actually increases with experience. On the whole, the wisest people are also the most humble because, in the heritage of Socrates, they have discovered that advancement involves the recognition of ignorance. A few years of real living can make any person realize that what we do not know far exceeds what we know.

Frequently, these days, I turn to the words of John Stuart Mill, who said that the world cannot too often remember that Socrates existed. This is one reason why I have installed a bust of the humble Athenian in my personal library. We do not know much about the early life of Socrates, except that he was a brave soldier. Possibly he was not always as humble as he showed himself to be at the end, when he saw clearly that the essence of wisdom is to know that we do not know.

Long after Socrates, it became essential to the Christian message to recognize that real freedom comes at the end of a process rather than at ·

the beginning. "If you continue in my word, you are truly my disciples, and you will know the truth, and the truth will make you free" (John 8:31-32, RSV). Plato had some intimation of this profound idea when, near the end of his final book, he wrote: "The learners themselves do not know what is learned to advantage until the knowledge which is the result of learning has found a place in the soul of each." Real freedom is something to be achieved, but it cannot be achieved cheaply. It comes at a price, and it is more a consequence than an antecedent. Only when the learning process is ended, or is ending, do we know what is learned. This is why authors often admit that they do not know what they are trying to say until they come to the end of the writing process. Because prefaces are usually written last, it is foolish for readers to omit them.

In the logic of living, gratitude is the normal result of humility. The more we realize that we are unworthy of our friends, the more grateful we tend to become. By a happy development of publishing, Cicero's famous essays on "Old Age" and "Friendship" are now bound together in one volume, as they should be. In earlier years we may not appreciate friendship, and sometimes we do not really value it until we have lost it. It is not a mere coincidence that makes us place our Thanksgiving celebration in the late autumn.

One of the noblest words in our language is *grace*, defined as "unearned blessing." We live by grace far more than by anything else. Accordingly, I find that one thing which I want to put into practice in my own life is the conscious and deliberate habit of finding somebody to thank. The person to thank may be the driver of the bus, the teller at the bank window, the church janitor, the policeman on the beat, the mail carrier, the clerk in the grocery store, the telephone operator, and many more. In this fashion, gratitude can become a way of life. The greatest blessing of maturity is that gratitude may transcend the single occasion, to become both habitual and continuous.

II
Persons

No species of writing seems more worthy of
cultivation than biography.

Samuel Johnson

"It is observed that a man improves more by reading the Story of a Person eminent for Prudence and Virtue, than by the finest Rules and Precepts of Morality." This is Joseph Addison at his brilliant best. With these words he began the 299th *Spectator*, on Tuesday, February 12, 1712, and they are as pertinent now as they were when Addison wrote them.

Because I believe the words quoted above, I have determined, in this collection of small essays, to stress persons more than anything else. Even the places mentioned in Part III and the institutions mentioned in Part IV receive most of their significance because of the persons who have been connected with them. Personality is vastly more important than geography can ever be because persons are superior to things and to all else that we know in God's universe. Very early in my professional life as a philosopher I became a Personalist, in the precise sense that I believe persons are the most important realities we can know. It became obvious to me that persons could not have arisen in an impersonal world, and this is my strongest single reason for believing that God really *is*. I cannot conceive of the existence of persons except in a world centered ultimately in a Person.

As I look back upon the course of my life I realize that my chief wealth has been that of friendship. It has been my privilege to know a number of people who have contributed generously to my own life; I have not deserved them, but I have nevertheless enjoyed them. Cicero, in his famous treatise on friendship, taught all who would listen how greatly we need one another. The wonder of sharing, he said, affects both joys and sorrows. Joys are increased by being shared, while sorrows are decreased by this amazing experience. "When fortune smiles on us," wrote Cicero, "friendship adds a luster to that smile; when she frowns, friendship absorbs her part and share of that frown, and thus makes it easier to bear." I really wish every person could write his autobiography because this act could facilitate the miracle of sharing. "I have often thought," said Dr. Johnson, "there has rarely passed a life of which a judicious and faithful narrative would not be useful."

The most powerful forces which we know are personal ones. *Human lives are changed by other lives.* As I look at my own life, after more than eighty years of learning, I realize that I have been showered by gifts which have come from many sources, nearly all of which are personal ones. Though I hesitate to write of "luck," honesty compels me to admit that I have been lucky, especially in my friendships. I have been associated with a number of persons whose companionship had aided me immensely in my Pilgrim's Progress. I have been surrounded by people who have shown me where some of the dangerous parts of the common journey are, telling me what I could never have learned alone.

It came to me as something of a discovery that many of the persons with whom I should like to be acquainted are approachable. In any case there is no harm in trying to meet persons from whom I believe I can learn. The conviction of the approachability of people who are leaders has been verified on numerous occasions. It has led to morning coffee with the Archbishop of Canterbury in London and to afternoon tea with Radhakrishnan in Madras. Why not? These are persons, too, and they may be as eager for friendship as anyone else. It was really a matter of surprise to me to realize that, if there was someone whom I wished to see, I could see him. That is why, when a group of us visit England this summer, we expect to have unhurried time with Lord Caradon, at the House of Lords in London, with Malcolm Muggeridge, near Tunbridge Wells, and with Bishop Stephen Neill in Oxford. The recognition that these are persons too, and that they have needs as we do, is a wonderfully liberating idea. Socrates believed that the same approach may be possible in life after death.

The number of individuals to whom I am indebted is, indeed, legion. Though some of them have been eminent in the eyes of the world, the vast majority of them have been inconspicuous. I am thinking now of the ones who have kept my library clean and neat, of those who have made airline reservations for me, of the printers who have put my words into type, of the waiters who have brought food to my table, of the private secretaries, of whom Robert Pitman has been chief, who have turned my handwritten manuscripts into what is fully legible. Any sensitive reader will be able to extend such a list and to realize that the list is never exhausted.

When this collection was planned it became obvious that, for reasons of space, it would be necessary to observe arbitrary limitations on the number to whom individual essays could be assigned. Soon the decision was made to limit the fifteen essays to persons meeting two qualifications. First, the individuals should be those with whom I have actually been acquainted; second, they should no longer be living. Only by this second qualification could I avoid making invidious distinctions.

By limiting the essays to those whom I have actually encountered in the flesh, I was saddened by the vast number eliminated. Because of the miracle of the written word it would be easy to write entire essays upon women and men whom I feel that I know, only because I have been enriched by their words. I wish I had time to write of Lancelot Andrewes, or of William Penn, or of John Milton. Unfortunately, all that I know about these people is what they wrote or what was written about them.

It is part of my good fortune, in my autumnal years, to spend the majority of my time in a library, an experience which I find both awesome and humbling. The experience of sitting daily among loved books is not fundamentally different from that of walking through a cemetery. In the library, the monuments are made only of paper, but they nevertheless serve the purpose of providing reminders of what ought not to be forgotten. In the cemetery the people of whom we are reminded are, for the most part, more humble in station than are those of whom we are reminded in a library; but they are not, for that reason, less important. A good case can be made for the practice of reading the death notices before anything else in the newspapers. President Wilbur thought that the most important part of any faculty meeting at Stanford was that devoted to memorials.

The fact that all to whom separate essays are assigned have already entered the next life does not mean that they are lacking in present and future effectiveness. Indeed, some of them now influence me far more than do any of my contemporaries. I learned long ago that a man wedded to his time will soon become a widower. I also know that a person has learned something of the meaning of life if he plants shade trees under which he knows full well that he will never sit. Indeed, on the very day in which these words are being written, I have actually helped plant young trees in front of my library.

As Horace taught us, there were brave men before Agamemnon. There were, also, wise men before Socrates, but they did not have the good fortune to be followed by students of the character of Plato, able and willing to keep their memories alive. I know that there have been spiritual giants outside the biblical tradition; but, unfortunately, most of them did not have the inestimable advantage of the written word. There may have been persons whose lives were as interesting as that of Samuel Johnson, but they did not have contact with any literary genius equal to that of James Boswell. There may have been intellectuals as brilliant as Blaise Pascal, but they lacked associates able to preserve and publish their *Pensées*.

The task of selecting a few from those who have gone on is so onerous that the outcome is almost arbitrary. Why have I not included Alexander Purdy, Henry J. Cadbury, William W. Comfort, William C. Dennis, Clarence Pickett, Herbert G. Wood, Anna Braithwaite Thomas, Elbert Russell, Henry Bartlett, Anna Brinton, or Augustus T. Murray, all of whom have belonged to my own spiritual fellowship? Why did I not include Mrs. David Starr Jordan or Amelia Gummere or

Margaret T. Carey? Each reader will have his own list and each will find selection difficult.

When we turn to the other excluded group, the persons arbitrarily omitted because they are still living, the problem is equally difficult. Why not include Edward Elson, long chaplain of the United States Senate? Why not include academic colleagues, such as Obert Tanner, who became my assistant at Stanford, and went on to a distinguished professorship at the University of Utah, or Landrum Bolling, who was my friend long before he was my president, or Dr. Paul Tournier, physician of Geneva and companion of sorrow in Athens, or John Wong, whose friendship began in Hong Kong, but continues now at Iowa State University, or Jan and Olga Erteszek, who represent the American story in an unparalleled fashion, or Harold Cope, who kept Friends University alive by his courageous determination not to accept defeat?

Whom can I omit without being patently unfair? I could, for example, have devoted an entire essay to Hans Roth, the photographer of Palo Alto, whom I first met in Birmingham, England, and who became our guest at Stanford when he migrated to America. The mention of Rodger Meier, of Dallas, could be justified. I wish I could devote an essay to Melita Fisher, of Woonsocket, Rhode Island, who is now nearly a century old, and who befriended me wonderfully at the start of my public career. I could easily justify the assignment of an entire essay to Tetsuo and Emily Kobayashi, who initiated Yokefellow work in Japan. A very special indebtedness is felt for Dr. William Orr, now librarian of Warner Pacific College of Portland, Oregon, who was the first director of the Yokefellow Academy, and for James Newby, the present director. It will be obvious to the perceptive reader that I have omitted all of those whose ties of intimacy are the closest. They will understand, with Plato, that the most important things cannot be said.

It is part of the wonder of friendship that each can add to the other's wealth in this regard. My hope is that because I mention certain people, whose memory I prize, I can encourage others to make their acquaintance. We cannot all be rich in money, but it is really not necessary that anyone should remain in intellectual poverty. By the magic of the written word, each person can choose his own companions and thereby enlarge the circle of friendship. If each reader succeeds in acquiring a few new friends, the entire effort is thereby justified.

1
John R. Mott

At the beginning of January 1920, there was held a Convention of the Student Volunteer Movement in Des Moines, attended by representatives of all of the major American colleges and universities. Being then in my sophomore year at Penn College, I attended as a representative of Penn, and profited from the experience. I thought of myself as in some sense a "student volunteer" and seriously considered missionary service in China. What helped me most was the opportunity to listen to strong Christian voices, the most effective of them being that of Dr. John R. Mott.

Dr. Mott was, in January 1920, fifty-four years of age and at the height of his powers. The Student Volunteer Convention, one of the most successful ever held, with 8,000 young men and women in attendance, drew from the brilliant leader the best that he had to give.

Though I did not meet Dr. Mott personally in 1920, I had the privilege of becoming a close friend and associate twenty years later, when both of us were members of the board of trustees of the Church Peace Union. Admiring the older man as I did, I often made it a point to sit by him at board meetings and to attempt to gain all that I could by his wisdom. When we became close associates, Mott had already become the acknowledged leader of the ecumenical forces of America, the World Student Federation, and the International Young Men's Christian Association. He was a genuine leader and he looked the part; but he never dominated the discussion. Later he was awarded the Nobel Prize for Peace.

Soon I learned something of the Mott story. After graduation from Cornell University the young John Mott became an effective leader in the student Y.M.C.A., with an unique ability to draw out the best from young men. Soon, a group of influential men, centered in New

York, made an unusual decision. They decided to pool their financial resources and to liberate Mott from the necessity of earning. From then until his death, more than a half-century later, no salary for Mott was ever required. He could travel anywhere in the world where he thought he ought to visit, especially in the world Christian Mission, and never worry about money, because the committee which had been formed took care of those expenses, as well as those connected with the support of his family. As late as 1947, when he was living in Florida and we invited him to Earlham to speak, I was mildly shocked by the fact that his visit required no travel reimbursement from us. When I asked Dr. Mott about it, his reply was, "It is cared for." It was then that, for the first time, I saw the unique letterhead, on which were the words: "The Committee for the Support of the Ministry of John R. Mott."

He was, indeed, engaged in a ministry, but he always took great satisfaction in his status as a lay Christian. Indeed, he chose as a title for his most influential book, *Liberating the Lay Forces of Christianity.* This volume, which was published in 1932, was the forerunner of many others dealing with the ministry of every Christian, regardless of secular occupation. I freely express my own indebtedness in this connection.

The last time I saw Dr. Mott was in August 1948, at Amsterdam, for the formation of the World Council of Churches. At eighty-three, the grand old man looked physically feeble, but he obviously took satisfaction from the concrete evidence of the ecumenicity for which he had worked and prayed so long. He was close to the end of his career and he seemed to know it. Later, in Washington, D.C., I had the privilege of dining with his widow, when we had a chance to think together of the extraordinary impact of one life.

John R. Mott may be known the longest for his motto: "The Evangelization of the World in This Generation." The fact that this dream did not materialize does not mean that it was false. *Mott knew as well as did anyone that the barriers to achievement were great, but he also knew that little is ever accomplished by low aims.* It is to his credit that he stirred the lives of countless persons, and particularly the young, who seemed to think that he was one of them.

The demonstration of tireless industry without the economic motive of survival is one of Mott's best contributions to our society. Being freed from earning, he worked harder than ever and he never stopped. He impels each of us to inquire what we might do if we were liberated as he was. Here is a major test of character.

2
Rufus M. Jones

Before I first saw Rufus Jones I was already keenly aware of his existence. I knew that he was the best-known member of New England Yearly Meeting, that he was highly influential in the Five Years Meeting, and that he had been the author of three volumes of the recently completed Rowntree Series of Quaker History. Our first meeting occurred in June 1923, at Moses Brown School in Providence, during the Yearly Meeting sessions. Rufus Jones was sixty years old, at the very height of his powers, and I was only twenty-two, but the difference in age soon seemed to be no barrier to our friendship. I little realized that, only ten years later, the generous man would invite me to be his junior colleague in the department of philosophy at Haverford College, serving with him daily during his final year of college teaching. Though I could not know the future, I rejoiced in the present.

Part of the excitement in the summer of 1923 arose from the fact that Dr. and Mrs. Jones had just returned from a sabbatical leave which included a visit to the Holy Land. After their stay in Providence they went to South China, Maine, where most of their summers were spent. With their travels behind them, Rufus and Elizabeth seemed very happy and relaxed, enjoying the presence of their daughter, Mary Hoxie, already enrolled at Mount Holyoke College.

The high point for me was the opportunity of engaging in walks on the Moses Brown campus with the man I highly esteemed. The contrast was extreme in every way. Professor Jones was the recipient of many honors and I of none. But, in spite of the contrast, Rufus appeared to pay attention to my part in the conversation, most of which bore on philosophical questions. He knew that I was a graduate of Penn College and never forgot that Penn was the first institution to grant him an honorary degree. He also knew that I had just completed a year of graduate study at Brown University, with which he had long had close connections. Some of the ideas which appeared in the good man's subsequent books, I was delighted to hear from his own lips at Providence.

One amusing event of the Yearly Meeting sessions of 1923 was that, during a summer storm, while Rufus was speaking at an evening session, all the lights were extinguished. Knowing nothing of the speaker's practice, I had no idea what he would do, but I soon recognized his resilience. With scarcely a pause, the speaker went right on, with a suitable interpolation to the effect that the incident was a good illustration of what happens to humans when they are cut off from their source of power.

The incident taught me much. I saw, better than I had seen before, the immense advantage of being so well prepared that speaking could proceed entirely without notes. I determined to follow this model. I learned, also, that a public speaker, if he is to be effective, must be able to adjust to new situations, changing course when conditions change.

When we spoke of preparation, my new friend often said he believed in being as fully prepared as possible and then also being as free as possible. I soon learned why he normally declined all social engagements for Saturday nights. The idea was to fill the mind as full as possible and then, after a good rest, speak out of the overflow.

I suppose that, prior to our first meeting, I had heard of the celebrated sense of humor which Rufus Jones exhibited, but I had not witnessed it. At Providence, however, I witnessed this abundantly. I think it was in 1923 that I first heard Rufus tell the joke on himself about the time, in his youth, when he tried to make an impression by using a few big words, such as "apocalyptic" and "eschatological." After he finished speaking an old lady arose to rebuke him, with the unforgettable words, "Our Lord said, 'Feed my lambs,' not 'my giraffes.'" Many of the stories were told with Maine dialect, made more amusing by the fact that he never lost its twang.

Our friendship lasted twenty-five years, until Dr. Jones died in 1948. When my first book was published in 1936 I had no difficulty in deciding to whom it would be dedicated; it was to Rufus Matthew Jones. When our little girl was born in 1941 we named her for Elizabeth, the wife of Rufus. If I get to heaven, I hope that one of my first visits will be with the man I first met in 1923.

3
Herbert C. Hoover

Though the time came when I saw a great deal of President and Mrs. Hoover, I actually knew their elder son before I knew his parents. This is because, when we both lived in Cambridge in the winter of 1927, our apartments were robbed by the same man. After the thief was apprehended, Herbert Hoover, Jr., and I became good friends by sitting together in a courtroom where we did not want to be. The friendship with my contemporary was renewed in Washington while he was Under Secretary of State, and was brought to a sad climax in Pasadena, when I conducted his memorial service.

The first association with the elder Hoovers came in 1929 when I shared in worship with them at the old Irving Street Meetinghouse in Washington. Later we were together at Florida Avenue after the new meetinghouse was built. My first visit to the White House was at the invitation of that gracious lady, Lou Henry Hoover.

When we settled on the campus of Stanford University in the summer of 1936, we counted it a privilege to live near the Hoovers, who owned the house which they later gave to the university as the president's home. When we began to have Friends meetings in our own Stanford home, the ex-president and his wife attended. Later their second son, Allan, joined them, along with his wife.

In our Stanford years the connections with the Hoovers were frequent and numerous. One day we went with them over the mountains to the coast where, facing the Pacific Ocean, we buried Tad Hoover's wife. When Mrs. Herbert Hoover died we were drawn together more closely, especially in the memorial service conducted in the Stanford chapel, which invoked the mood of celebration. Her burial was arranged to make it easy to move her body to West Branch, Iowa, where it was taken after the burial of her husband.

The most moving of all of our connections was that which came when President Hoover died, in October 1964. The time, as far as we were concerned, was highly inconvenient because my wife and I were on a freighter ship between Hong Kong and Saigon, when the sorrowful news was cabled to us. There was no chance to start home until the ship completed its tortuous course up the Saigon River and the air flight could begin. This delay meant that we missed the services in both St. Bartholomew's Church of New York, and the Rotunda in the United States Capitol, but we arrived at West Branch in time for the climactic event. We were impressed when, in the procession, we observed people standing at attention on the road from the Cedar Rapids airport to the village which was our destination. To our amazement, 75,000 people were gathered between the simple birth-place and the place of burial. Fortunately the weather was ideal in every way.

The difficulty of the long journey to West Branch was more than justified. I kept thinking of the years which this good man had devoted to child feeding, of the splendid example of family life which the Hoovers provided, of the selfless service to the nation, always without salary. I thought also of the way in which he had been maligned, when he was blamed personally for an economic storm that was really world-wide, and I was glad that I could do a little to help to restore a just balance. When the memorial service was over, we flew to Los Angeles with the Hoover family and then proceeded on to Southeast Asia, where we joined the freighter tour after an absence of only seven days.

Today it is possible to visit the little hill, near President Hoover's birthplace, and to stand at the beautiful spot where the bodies of Herbert and Lou Hoover rest. They represent a growth in which the Quaker roots have made a difference. I am grateful for the fact that their lives have touched mine.

4
Alfred North Whitehead

It was my good fortune to listen to Professor Whitehead early in his American career, when he delivered, in Boston, the Lowell Lectures, "Religion in the Making." The four lectures delivered in February 1926 attracted a large company of listeners. Because of his original work in the field of logic and his broad understanding of both ethics and science, Whitehead was already famous when he emigrated from England to America in 1924; but it was in our country that the good man came into the fullness of his powers. When he died in 1947, at the age of eighty-six, he was widely perceived as the most eminent philosopher of the century. It is no wonder, therefore, that, as a very young man, I considered it a privilege to listen to his eloquent discourse.

Though I did not meet Professor Whitehead personally in 1926, my opportunity to meet him came in a fortunate fashion in December 1944. At that time, enjoying a semisabbatical leave from my duties at Stanford University, I was appointed by Harvard University to teach the philosophy of religion. Since Professor Whitehead was then almost eighty-four years old, and fully retired from the teaching of philosophy, I assumed that there was not much chance of meeting him. But one day, while I was staying at Lowell House, I received a telephone call and, to my surprise, the voice was that of the famous man himself. He asked me to be his guest at a dinner arranged by the Society of Junior Fellows. Delighted to be able to accept the invitation, I sat by Whitehead as we dined. It seemed the chance of a lifetime.

In his last few years Professor Whitehead, conscious of declining energy, gave up everything else except the nurture of young men. When I dined with him, the aged scholar was so frail that he had to spend the entire day in bed in order to conserve strength for the evening engagement. Like Socrates, he knew that he could not do much, but he was determined to concentrate on the encouragement of the young, who might be able to carry on when he could do no more.

In the course of our conversation I said, "I suppose that the real purpose of this gathering is that those of us who are younger may be able to profit by contact with our elders and betters." Immediately he replied, "Oh, not at all, not at all! If anyone thought that he was an elder or better, he would not be an elder or better." This highly quotable remark was characteristic of his style. More than any person I have met, he spoke almost constantly in aphorisms. Aphorisms so abound in his published writings that he has become one of the most quoted of contemporary authors. What I suddenly realized that evening in Eliot House was that the style of the man's writing was essentially the style of his speech.

Already, in 1926, I had noticed how quotable the philosopher was. It was in "Religion in the Making" that he said, "I hazard the prophecy that religion will conquer which can render clear to popular understanding some eternal greatness incarnate in the passage of temporal fact." *By this he meant that effective religion is never some separated experience, but is, instead, the kind that makes a difference in common life.* Very early I made this idea central to my own understanding of how the Christian faith can be revitalized. Partly because of what the good man taught, I saw that the validity of any faith is expressed not merely in how people worship, but even more by how they work, and how they love one another.

Of all of the quotable sentences produced by Alfred North Whitehead the most famous is that concerning education, and especially education which includes values. *"Moral education,"* he said in 1929, *"is impossible apart from the habitual vision of greatness."* Thus, at the age of sixty-eight, the philosopher may rightly be said to have reached the highest point of his long career. All along, he had seen deliberate mediocrity as the enemy of civilization, but he had never expressed his convictions so well before. *Unless education has moral content,* he was convinced, *it is little more than "scraps of information."*

Always the purpose of the teacher must be to "shed details in favor of principles."

One of the chief contributions of Professor Whitehead to all of us is the enlarged conception of how productive the later years of a well-conducted life may be. When he gave up his prestigious British professorship at the age of sixty-three, he might have, according to the conventional expection of retirement, done virtually nothing; but the completion of one set of tasks was, in his view, only the beginning of others. He lived twenty-three years as an American scholar, producing his most important books in the brilliant autumn of his life. Here his beloved Plato, who produced *The Laws* at the age of eighty, was his pattern, the years immediately following the conclusion of his Harvard professorship in 1936 being the most productive of his entire career. The fact that Alfred North Whitehead touched my life, however briefly, is something for which I am profoundly grateful.

5
Harry Emerson Fosdick

Much about Harry Emerson Fosdick was known to me long before I enjoyed my first visit with him. The connection began when, as a college student in the early 1920s, I read his book *The Meaning of Prayer.* In spite of the excellence of many later productions, my opinion is that this particular book was never surpassed by the gifted preacher-author. It was this early volume which introduced me to some of the most famous of all written prayers, including a few from the pen of Dr. Samuel Johnson.

Like many other Americans, I listened to Dr. Fosdick as he gave countless sermons on national radio; and I was glad to learn of his friendship with John D. Rockefeller, Jr., which led to the building of Riverside Church in New York. Like millions of others, I learned to sing the new hymn which Dr. Fosdick composed for the dedication of Riverside Church, "God of Grace, and God of Glory." I was thrilled to know that a hymn of such obvious excellence could be produced in our generation, and I liked the hymn even more when it was matched with the haunting Welsh tune, CWM RHONDDA.

Our first meeting came in the tower of Riverside Church when we were together for a glorious half-hour. Because I had heard that the famous preacher, though a loyal Baptist, had a strong and growing affection for Friends, I decided to invite him to join the Wider Quaker Fellowship. He accepted the invitation at once and remained a part of the Fellowship until his death.

One evidence of Dr. Fosdick's ecumenical spirit was his great admiration for Rufus M. Jones. Well aware that thousands who might profit from the thinking of Rufus Jones would never be exposed to one of his books, Fosdick decided to produce an anthology of the writings of his admired friend, calling the book *Rufus Jones Speaks to Our Time*

(Macmillan, 1951). As in so many other areas of thought, the importance of sensing what time it is became uppermost. Dr. Fosdick freely confessed that the book by Dr. Jones entitled *Social Law in the Spiritual World* "opened the door to a new era" in his early life when he was just entering the ministry. Accordingly, the editor understood what one of Professor Jones' students meant when he said of his beloved teacher, "He lighted my candle." Part of Fosdick's success as an anthologist was that he appreciated the humor of Dr. Jones. One incident which he especially loved concerned the critic who prayed before Rufus Jones spoke, saying, "Thou knowest, O Lord, that we are about to hear a great many things that are not so."

Our closest connection arose in his effort to find a title for his completed autobiography. What drew us together was the fact that both of us published with the House of Harper and had the same editor, the able Eugene Exman, who saw publishing as a ministry. Though Fosdick's autobiography was complete in the autumn of 1954, he could not, try as he might, come up with a title. Eugene Exman accordingly turned to me, asking me to try.

My search began at once with the typed and titleless book in front of me. Quickly I decided that, if it were possible, we ought to employ Fosdick's own words, rather than mine. Why not search for the right words in the already famous hymn? I looked for a long time at the phrase, "Grant us wisdom, Grant us courage, For the facing of this hour." Could "The Facing of This Hour" be the title? No, it could not, because the reference was frankly temporary, whereas the book in front of me covered a very wide span. Next, I turned to the stanza reading "Grant us wisdom, Grant us courage, For the living of these days." So great was the impact of these lines, that I jumped right out of my chair. Here indeed was a superb title, and it was indeed Dr. Fosdick's own, *The Living of These Days*.

Harper's arranged a luncheon in New York, so that two of their authors could have an unhurried time together, and, during the luncheon, I proposed the title which the good man accepted almost at once. When the book was published in 1956, Dr. Fosdick graciously told in his Preface the story of the selection of the title.

Later, I found it a moving experience to be invited to preach from Fosdick's pulpit at Riverside Church. What moved me most deeply, however, was the opportunity to sit in the little room where the good man had sat so often before facing the congregation with a message. I thank God that our lives have overlapped and that Fosdick still speaks to us.

6
Edith Hamilton

The voyage from Liverpool to New York on the *Britannic* in 1958 was made memorable to me by new friendships. It will not be a surprise to my readers to be told that my first act, after embarkation, was an examination of the passenger list, in order to see whether there were persons on board from whom I might learn. Since the names of Paul Tillich and Edith Hamilton struck me forcibly, I spent several hours on deck with both of these remarkable persons. Though both of my new friends were easily approachable, it was with Edith Hamilton that I spent the most time. She had already received the signal honor, on her ninetieth birthday, of being made an honorary citizen of Athens, with a key to the city.

My visits with Edith Hamilton were only two, but they were sufficient to make a deep impression upon my life. As a Hoosier, I was proud to think of Edith Hamilton as growing up in Fort Wayne. The story of her girlhood, as she told it more than twenty years ago, is as vivid as if I had heard it only yesterday. Her father, sensing the danger of mediocrity, and believing that school might hold them back from the development of which they were capable, never allowed his daughters to go to school. Accordingly, he taught them himself, with primary stress upon the Latin language. When Edith was only seven years old, this Indiana businessman gave her exactly six weeks in which to master Caesar's *Gallic Wars*, with the surprising result that the girl, young as she was, actually did the work.

When I made the obvious remark that she was smarter than other girls, Miss Hamilton replied by saying, "On the contrary, I was more stupid than others. In fact, I was so stupid that I didn't know but what I had to do it." By the age of thirteen she had mastered Greek sufficiently to read Plato's *Dialogues* in the original and, what is even more remarkable, to read these for pleasure. The Hamilton story bears directly upon the modern philosophy of education in that many students do less than their best, chiefly because they are not challenged by high standards of expectation.

Without ever being in school a single day, Edith Hamilton entered Bryn Mawr College, from which she received both B.A. and M.A. degrees in 1894. After further study in Germany, she helped to found Bryn Mawr School for Girls, in Baltimore, becoming headmistress. Following early retirement in 1922, the brilliant woman used her forty remaining years to establish herself as an author, winning fame first with her book *The Greek Way.* It was because I had read this book that I was impelled to seek out the author as soon as I learned that we were fellow passengers.

The book made me realize keenly that the primary task of those who care about culture is the restoration of roots. The key sentence, I soon realized, was as follows:

> Athens had entered upon her brief and magnificent flowering of genius which so molded the world of mind and of spirit that our mind and spirit are today different.

It was a special blessing to be able to meet with the writer in her own home not long before her death, which occurred at the age of ninety-five. My wife and I were able to do this because, in 1961, we were spending two weeks as guests of Wesley Seminary in Washington, not far from the Hamilton home on Massachusetts Avenue. Though we shall never forget the warm manner in which we were received by the gracious lady, what we remember most is the occupation in which she was engaged as we entered her living room. The floor around her chair was covered with proof sheets of her introductions to the *Dialogues of Plato,* scheduled to appear soon in the Bollingen Series. When, in my own library, I look at the volume now, I think of the elderly woman whom we caught reading proof. We were sure of at least one thing; she did not waste her limited time.

Our own lives were enriched as we conversed with a person who had lived her entire life dedicated to the vision of excellence and for whom retirement, far from being an occasion for boredom, was an opportunity to do what had not been done earlier. As we sat in her house, she told how she expected to visit Germany during the following summer. She was planning this trip at the age of ninety-four, she said, because she wished to revisit some of the scenes of her German graduate study and to visit other places for the first time. In short, she was determined to live, as long as she lived.

7
Eli Lilly

Until February 1946, Eli Lilly was almost unknown to me. I knew something of the famous pharmaceutical firm which bears the name, but little of the philanthropy and nothing of the man himself. We met first at a dinner sponsored by Wabash College in the Columbia Club of Indianapolis. By good fortune I mentioned, in my dinner address, a forthcoming visit to Germany under the direction of the Friends Ambulance Unit. At the close of the dinner, Mr. Lilly approached me saying he wished to send, as part of my luggage, several thousand dollars' worth of vitamin tablets, to help in supplementing the diet of the German people then known, in the months immediately following the war, to be poor.

Of course, I was pleased to have even a small part in such generosity, but did not realize that the experience would lead ultimately to a valued friendship.

After beginning my teaching duties at Earlham in the autumn of 1946, the time came for visits to Eli Lilly, along with President Thomas E. Jones, seeking funds for the erection of the new buildings which were constructed in that period. In each case we told Mr. Lilly what we were trying to accomplish at the college and soon discovered that he was glad to participate in a program which sought to combine, in one pattern, Christian commitment and academic excellence. One high point in this effort came when we told our Indianapolis friend of the need to replace Earlham Hall, which was so decayed that it was actually dangerous. Needing a million and a half dollars for the replacement, we summoned all the courage we had and asked him whether he would provide one-third of the amount, if we would raise the remainder. To our immense relief, the proposal was accepted and the new central building of the college was constructed two decades ago.

Eli Lilly's philanthropy, which supported so many good causes, was carried on both with his personal funds and through the Lilly Endowment, of which he was always a board member. It was through the endowment that the first serious funding of the Yokefellow Movement was accomplished. In a similar way the Lillys helped to pay for the construction of the Yokefellow Institute and the Lilly Library on the Earlham Campus. In many instances, the endowment made the first suggestion of a gift, without waiting for any request. This was particularly true of the Yokefellow Prison Ministry for which, at the first, Lillys provided the entire support.

As our friendship ripened, Mr. Lilly and I had regular appointments for lunch, always in the dining room of the new Lilly building of Indianapolis. Each luncheon was made mildly amusing by the modesty of the good man's menu. On all occasions Mr. Lilly ordered pie *a la mode* and nothing else. At first I felt ashamed of myself for ordering more, but my host sought to put my mind at ease by explaining that he found pie with ice cream was good for him, but since he could not afford the calories of this *in addition* to a regular lunch, he omitted the ordinary items. He went on to say that, after all, he was not a growing child, that a complete balance might not therefore be required, and that his slight indulgence was surely not very wrong.

The standing joke about the pie *a la mode* was representative of the essential modesty of Eli Lilly's life. He knew that he was an old man, with only a few years to live at best, and he sought to live the final years as productively as possible. After the death of his wife and his only child, Mr. Lilly was a lonely man. Grateful for the wealth bestowed on him by business success, he found this was by no means sufficient for the fullness of life to which he felt called.

One surprising enlargement of Eli Lilly's life came about by his literary activity. In 1957 there was published his impressive volume, *History of the Little Church on the Circle,* an account of the development over a period of 117 years of Christ Church Parish, Indianapolis. Of this parish Eli Lilly was a faithful and generous member, and in the building which he loved his memorial service was held. This prominent though essentially modest building on the Circle of Indianapolis is now the Cathedral Church of the Diocese of Indiana.

In the history of the local Episcopal church, Eli Lilly came to one outstanding conclusion, to the effect that "leadership is the pearl without price." He discovered that the quality of the public ministry was the crucial factor in spiritual effectiveness. Under some pastors, he observed, there is "an upsurge in the life and vitality of the church," and with others, this did not occur, even though the members remained the same.

Another of Eli Lilly's literary ventures was a book called *Schliemann in Indianapolis,* an account of one phase in the life of the famous archeologist who uncovered ancient Troy and discovered the shaft graves of Mycenae. In short, our valued friend, far from being satisfied with making money, reached out in many directions. He was extremely pleased with the part played by his firm in overcoming polio; he took a deep interest in the colleges; and he sought to lift as many burdens as could be lifted in one short life.

8
Dwight D. Eisenhower

My first acquaintance with President Dwight D. Eisenhower was wholly unexpected. The President, convinced that the United States, in its self-portraiture before the world, did not express adequately or clearly its spiritual roots, turned to the U.S. Information Agency and to its auxiliary, The Voice of America, in the effort to correct what he perceived as a distortion. What he desired was a new program to be expressed in a variety of ways, including the selection of books for American libraries in foreign countries and broadcasts in foreign languages. My original telephone call from Washington on this subject came in January 1954, as I was completing a semester of teaching at Earlham and was free to serve elsewhere for several months. When the position was offered, I accepted it gladly, hoping thereby to make my contribution to the creation of peace.

When my work with the United States Information Agency began in Washington in February 1954, I had never seen President Eisenhower face to face, but this soon changed. The quick change came when I was invited to preach the sermon at the National Presbyterian Church, with the Eisenhowers in attendance. Soon after this, I visited the President in the Oval Office, where he told me something of the personal faith by which he sought to live. I was struck by the calmness with which he could face the multitude of decisions facing him daily, and soon saw that much of the secret of the calmness lay in his strong sense of the guiding hand of God. Like Abraham Lincoln, he felt that his chief relationship to Almighty God was instrumental.

The deep spiritual roots of the Eisenhower family were those of a very modest people, the River Brethren. In almost constant movement around the world for several decades, the Eisenhowers had no settled church membership until they joined the National Presbyterian Church in Washington; but the pattern of the plain people was a constant source of strength. The great man was never ashamed of his origins.

One of the main pillars of spiritual strength of the Eisenhower family was the President's mother. The level of her personal humility is represented by a story which I often heard and finally was able to verify by asking Milton Eisenhower, the President of Johns Hopkins University. The younger brother of the President vouched for the story as entirely true, as follows: The elder Mrs. Eisenhower was traveling by train during the period of the war when her gifted son was Supreme Commander of the Allied forces. On the train she sat next to another woman passenger who had no idea of the older woman's identity and took advantage of the opportunity to talk endlessly about her son, telling proudly how he had been made a corporal. Finally, a bit ashamed of dominating the conversation so long, the stranger said to Mrs. Eisenhower, "Tell me about your son." The entire reply of the humble lady was, "He's in the army too."

After the conclusion of the years in the White House, when the Eisenhowers lived at Gettysburg, I was privileged to visit the ex-President there. In those days he spent most of his time in quarters provided by Gettysburg College, thereby protecting the privacy of family life. Though holding no public office, he was as concerned as ever with the problems of the nation, including the moral problems. He illustrated, almost perfectly, the conception that, though a good person may retire from a position, he or she cannot retire from a commitment.

As we look back now on the eight years of the presidency of Dwight D. Eisenhower, we look with gratitude. The paradox is that the man of military genius was able to produce an atmosphere of peace and order. The absence of damaging inflation now seems to us almost too good to be true. The word "Vietnam" was not yet a part of our general vocabulary, and damaging troubles in the colleges had not appeared. The world, of course, was not perfect, but it was amazingly orderly. We can see now that part of the reason for the sense of order was the character of the man who occupied the highest office.

We understand better the effectiveness of President Eisenhower as a leader when we try to see clearly what his vision of America was. He saw the danger inherent in a posture of boastfulness about either our power or our economic achievements. He did not want his beloved country to be satisfied with material success. Indeed, he realized that, if material success is all that we have, the time will come when we have it no longer. This is why he took satisfaction in the addition of the phrase "Under God" to the salute to the flag. This was the more meaningful to him because of his residence at Gettysburg and the fact that it was at the Gettysburg Battlefield that President Lincoln added the inspired phrase to the consciousness of the nation.

Though Eisenhower did not have the same gift of eloquence that Lincoln demonstrated, he understood what it means to say "under God." We cannot know all that Lincoln meant when, on November 19, 1863, he made the fortunate interpolation of the now familiar phrase; but we do know that he was seeking to express a nonidolatrous patriotism. Fortunately, this is what the thirty-fourth President likewise sought. We remember him with gratitude.

9
Reinhold Niebuhr

One of the most agreeable dividends produced by my position at Stanford University was that of becoming well acquainted with Professor Reinhold Niebuhr, who gave the West Lectures in the winter of 1944. The possibility of close acquaintance was facilitated by my appointment by President Wilbur as chairman of the lecture committee. The prospect of the lectureship was an exciting one, partly because Niebuhr had, by that time, reached the apex of his national reputation. At the age of fifty-one he was sought as a speaker, particularly in universities. One result of his reputation was that his set of West Lectures drew capacity crowds, the largest since the inauguration of the lectureship. The very title of the 1944 West Lectures was intriguing, *The Children of Light and the Children of Darkness*. It was Niebuhr's intention to provide a vindication of democracy and a critique of its traditional defense.

The students, professors, and townspeople who listened to Reinhold Niebuhr with keen anticipation were not disappointed. His lectures sparkled with insights which have been widely quoted ever since. The most quoted of his aphorisms was "Man's capacity for justice makes democracy possible; but man's inclination to injustice makes democracy necessary." Though our distinguished visitor spoke in extempore style, I had the advantage of pretty well knowing what he was going to say because I had a copy of his manuscript on my lap as I sat in the audience.

We had other opportunities to appreciate the wit and wisdom of our new friend because of conversation at dinners and his brilliant performance in dialogue with small groups. It was in one of these groups that Niebuhr intensified my determination to give serious consideration to the theology of Abraham Lincoln. In a planned discussion a professor asked our visitor who the most original theologian of America might be; and, without any hesitation, Niebuhr replied, "Abraham Lincoln." The members of the group were surprised because they naturally expected reference to some person occupying an academic post, but all soon realized that a person could be a genuine theologian without having a professional claim to being one. If a theologian is one who has a knowledge of God, there must be many who occupy no professional positions yet justify the use of the noble term. It may be that I should never have engaged in long study of Lincoln's religious thinking, had it not been for Niebuhr's laconic answer to a question, long ago.

Reinhold Niebuhr grew up in the tradition of German American intellectuals. Steeped in the Evangelical tradition, he studied in Elmhurst College in Illinois and Eden Theological Seminary, St. Louis, and later received the degree of B.D. at Yale Divinity School. The Yale experience was important in his development because it provided liberation from the sectarian limitations of his early youth. Soon he became pastor of a congregation in Detroit, where he felt keenly the crosscurrents of social and economic life in the boom atmosphere of a new and powerful industry. Some of the ideas which were formed in his Detroit days were published later in a book entitled *Leaves from the Notebook of a Tamed Cynic.*

Because of the widening reputation achieved in Detroit Niebuhr was offered a position on the faculty of Union Seminary, New York, becoming Professor of Applied Christianity in 1930. While in New York he soon became the most influential theologian of the United States, affecting in a remarkable way the whole climate of opinion, so far as religion was concerned. Along with distinguished colleagues, he helped to make Union Seminary a place of continuous intellectual vitality.

My first contact with Professor Niebuhr occurred in March 1929, when I was one of his listeners as he gave a public address during the sessions of Philadelphia Yearly Meeting of Friends. Still new in New York, the speaker's ideas were not well known, and it is only fair to say that many of those who heard him at the Arch Street Meetinghouse were deeply shocked. Already he had renounced the kind of liberalism which talks of the natural goodness of man. He had come to see that no philosophy can stand unless it comes to terms with the profound idea of sin. Early as it was in his career, Niebuhr was already expressing many of the convictions which were matured by the time of his famous Gifford Lectures, "The Nature and Destiny of Man." Unless the ubiquity of sin is recognized, he believed, no sound philosophy of human life can be even proposed. He saw vividly how sin, in the precise sense of self-centeredness and the struggle for power, enters into every human situation and is, therefore, something with which we must always reckon. Sin emerges, he affirmed, even in the life of the church.

The friendship established in California in 1944 did not end there, but continued in a variety of ways. One connection which I prized was my new friend's strong support of my first small book *The Predicament of Modern Man*. The fact that he thought highly of the book, and that Harper used his words on the dust jacket, undoubtedly added materially to the number of readers. For this I am grateful, because the wide readership which ensued opened many other doors to me.

10
Edward Gallahue

My first acquaintance with Edward Gallahue came about as a result of my delivery of a sermon at North Methodist Church in Indianapolis one Sunday morning more than thirty years ago. In the afternoon of that day my wife and I were entertained in the Gallahue home in the northern part of the city. Today I have no idea what I said in the sermon, but I can never forget the discussion in the afternoon. Mr. Gallahue had already read a few of my books, particularly *The Logic of Belief.* He told us how, with his effort to overcome boyhood poverty, he had not had sufficient time or energy to give adequate attention to the spiritual quest which was, he realized, his first love. Because of what I had written, he hoped that our new friendship might be productive of some clarity in his conclusions about the most important questions that human beings ever face. I discovered later that the invitation to give the sermon at North Church had come at Mr. Gallahue's suggestion.

His story was a vivid one. I learned that day of Ed's poor start. Although eager to learn, he had not been able, he said, to go to college, but, instead, had worked to support his mother. Very little help of any kind had been provided by his inadequate father. In spite of this poor start Ed had, in conjunction with his brother, Dudley, originated the American States Insurance Company. This company prospered in spite of the lack of capital, chiefly because it was one of the first financial institutions to specialize in automobile coverage. By the time we first met, Ed Gallahue had achieved financial security, had built a fine home in a favorable location, and had married. My first visit to Ed and Dorothy Gallahue's home came soon after the birth of their daughter. Outwardly, Ed Gallahue's career was a success, and he might have been expected to take his ease, but this was what he could not do. To try to find answers to his most insistent questions, Ed collected a fine library which he housed in a beautifully paneled room in his Indianapolis home. As I studied his collection on the occasion of our first encounter, I soon noticed that his keenest interest lay in the books dealing with philosophy and religion. For example, I noted that he owned nearly all of the volumes written by Harry Emerson Fosdick. When I told my host that I knew Dr. Fosdick personally, the interest quickened noticeably.

As a result of his voracious reading of philosophical and religious literature, Ed Gallahue realized that he was a believer, but he saw that genuine religious belief is never adequate apart from a fellowship. This fellowship, he saw, was the church. Never having been affiliated with any church, my host, as he repeated the story, studied as many forms of the church, both Protestant and Catholic, as he could, and decided finally to seek membership in the Methodist denomination. In cold logic, he made his decision without any emotional ties. What drew him to Methodism, he said, was its splendid organization, combined with its record of human service. Living in Indianapolis all of his life he could not fail, for example, to be keenly aware of the great Methodist Hospital of that city. Once he had made his general decision, he applied to North Church for actual membership, largely because of the geographical proximity of its physical resources. He developed, very early, a close friendship with the resident Methodist bishop, Richard Raines, providing the bishop with valuable business advice and generous financial support. Ed knew from the beginning that it was a matter of integrity to put his financial resources where his religious commitment was.

Because our Sunday afternoon visit was clearly only a beginning, we arranged more opportunities to engage in intellectual dialogue. I soon saw that this interested my friend much more than did the business success which he had already achieved. Ed was the first to suggest to me that, in order to reach the minds of contemporary men and women, we needed really new approaches. He was always looking for new wineskins to contain the new wine. He early suggested the incorporation of what later became Yokefellows International and even arranged for his own attorney to draw up the original charter, with bylaws. Saying that there would be inevitable expenses, such as postage and travel, he handed to me one thousand dollars. Before he died, Mr. Gallahue had the satisfaction of knowing that the movement he had helped to originate was firmly established. He was a member of the first Yokefellow board of trustees.

More and more the Gallahues made visits to Richmond, taking a deep interest in the development of the house on College Avenue which was the scene of the first Yokefellow Retreats. The connection was rendered closer by the fact that my chief partner in the leadership of the early Retreats was Ed's dearest friend, Bishop Raines. An unexpected consequence of the valued friendship was Mr. Gallahue's decision to build the Teague Library, for my use as long as I live, and in honor of his mother, representing the Teague family.

11
Thomas R. Kelly

When I terminated my teaching at Haverford College in the summer of 1936, I created, incidentally, an opportunity for a man who needed precisely what Haverford had to offer. This was Thomas Kelly, who became my successor in the philosophy department, and who remained in this agreeable post until his untimely death. When the new opportunity arose, he was teaching in the University of Hawaii where he enjoyed his work, which included creative contacts with Far Eastern cultures. Pleasant as the life in Hawaii was, Tom Kelly felt sure that there was another chapter in his career, which he hoped would be on the eastern seaboard. He liked the Haverford scene which he had experienced earlier as a graduate student, and he adored Rufus Jones, still vigorous at seventy-three. The fact that I was leaving Haverford seemed to provide exactly the opportunity desired. President Comfort arranged the new appointment by mail and the best years of Tom Kelly began. No one could see that, within a few years, following his death, the name of Thomas Kelly would be known by thousands who never saw him.

In the late summer of 1937, we returned from California to the Philadelphia area for the Friends World Conference, which was held at Haverford and Swarthmore, and which I had the privilege of addressing. This gave me an opportunity to converse with my successor, with whom I had not previously had much direct acquaintance. This contact in 1937 was an important step in the unfolding of the drama because it opened the way for the publication of essays which later, in book form, made Thomas Kelly famous. Having continued the editorship of *The Friend* in spite of my removal to California, I was always watching for new material of excellence. Though Richard Wood did the day-by-day work of assembling the fortnightly magazine, he depended upon me to solicit articles, a task which could be done in California as easily as in Pennsylvania. The recent introduction of airmail made this operation possible. In this role I corresponded with Thomas Kelly, who agreed that *The Friend* might provide him with the ideal means of disseminating his new and exciting ideas.

The Kelly story is the story of radical conversion. Before the radical change in December 1937, he had been a good man and a good teacher of philosophy, both at Earlham and elsewhere; but by the start of the year 1938, he exhibited a new passion previously unobserved. It was as though a new fire had been lighted in the man. He collected a small band of students who met in the Kelly home and who became ignited as their mentor was. His public messages took on a totally new urgency, and everything about him burned with a fierce new flame. Almost as though he knew how short the time was, he used it with a terrible urgency. In the deepest sense of the word, he had experienced a religious conversion, not unlike that of John Wesley at Aldersgate two hundred years before. Suddenly, at the end of the year 1937, Kelly had the unmistakable sense of God as reaching out to him. The response was what he called "Holy Obedience."

One causal element in the new burst of vitality was an experience of failure at Harvard, where it was expected that he would receive the Ph.D. degree. He had completed his doctoral dissertation, devoted to a French philosopher, Emile Meyerson, and had done all of the course work required; but to the amazement of many he failed to pass the final oral examination for which he sat in the autumn of 1937. At last the chairman of the examiners announced to Thomas Kelly that he had failed and that he could not return. This was a heartbreaking experience; but, paradoxically, it became a redemptive force in the good man's life. The greatest achievements of Thomas Kelly's life came *after* his greatest personal disappointment. In sober fact, tragedy was turned into victory!

Kelly's radical change from secular philosophy to profound religious experience is indicated by his essay "The Eternal Now and Social Concern," which showed that Kelly, at the age of 44, had finally arrived. The brilliant essay, published in *The Friend* March 24, 1938, was followed a year later by "The Simplification of Life," dated March 23, 1939.

Thomas Kelly never saw the book which made his name well known because the very idea of publishing his essays did not arise until after his death. A number of people, of whom Douglas Steere was the most active, saw soon after Thomas Kelly's death, January 17, 1941, that his spiritual writings ought to reach a wider circle of readers. Accordingly, Professor Steere, Kelly's colleague and mine, arranged with Eugene Exman of the House of Harper to bring out a collection of essays, to which they attached the fortunate title *Testament of Devotion*. Douglas Steere agreed to provide a biographical introduction, and the book was published when the deceased author's name was almost entirely unknown except in a few Quaker Centers. To the amazement of those who undertook this publishing challenge, the book rapidly became a best-seller. After numerous printings the volume is still in demand, having been added, by many readers, to the small list of Christian Classics of Devotion. What Harper thought was a gamble has turned out to be a publishing success.

12
John Baillie

Though long familiar with the brilliant writings of John Baillie, my personal acquaintance with him was limited to one year, 1948. In that year I was with him on three occasions. The first opportunity to know the Scottish theologian was on shipboard, going from New York to Southampton, when we could enjoy friendly conversations on deck. The second chance to be with him came in Edinburgh, when I gave the Tercentenary Lecture, in honor of Robert Barclay, in the Assembly Hall of the Church of Scotland. It pleased me that Professor Baillie did me the honor of attending the lecture and of chatting with me afterward. The third and the most satisfying encounter occurred at Amsterdam, when, along with Donald Baillie of St. Andrews University, we were lodged in the same small hotel and enjoyed breakfast together for nine days.

In his public career, which included service in Canada and the United States as well as his native Scotland, Dr. Baillie established a firm reputation as one who combined, without confusion or embarrassment, a simple Christian faith with a powerful intellect. He helped me by his demonstration of the possibility of uniting tough-mindedness and tender-mindedness in one character. The two aspects of his life were so closely associated that it was hard to decide the right order of adjective and noun. Was Baillie an evangelical intellectual or a rational evangelical?

It was said, after John Baillie's death, that there were three pieces of furniture in his personal library that, together, epitomized his personality. One was the desk where he habitually sat for hours, developing and refining his ideas as he put them on paper. Some of his books, particularly his Gifford Lectures on religious experience, demanded extremely close attention to the logical development of the profound ideas. He knew that lectures such as he prepared never come easily, though the style makes them easy to read. Above all, in his writing, he strove for clarity, knowing that fogginess is always an evidence that the final work of thinking and writing has not been done.

The second piece of revelatory furniture was the big upholstered chair, which he occupied nearly every afternoon when he was at Edinburgh, his chief purpose being conversation with the numerous people who came in an endless stream to solicit his advice about their own lives. Many of these were young men, particularly from Canada, the United States, South Africa, and Australia. They came because of what they had read in his books or heard in his public addresses and sermons. The total effect which Dr. Baillie achieved by this friendly ministry cannot be measured, but we know that it was very great. No visitor ever had reason to feel that his coming was an imposition. Habitually, the professor would rise as a visitor came to the door and stride across the room to welcome him.

The third significant furnishing of the room was a kneeling pad by the window, where Dr. Baillie knelt every day to pray. Because the discipline of regularity in prayer was important to him, his devotional life was never hit and miss. Near the prayer pad were several different translations of the Scriptures and a few of the Christian Classics of Devotion. These are reflected in his own printed prayers.

The three sides of Baillie's life did not exist in separate compartments, but influenced one another. He knew that it was required of him to *think*, to *serve*, and to *pray*, and that each of these vocations was part of a whole calling.

In the long run John Baillie may be remembered longest for his own devotional book, *A Diary of Private Prayer*, which is rapidly achieving the status of a classic. Though radically different from his philosophical and theological works, it is as carefully prepared as they are, and bears the marks of meticulous revision.

Baillie was keenly aware of the important difference between discussion *about* God and direct communication *with* God. Prayer he saw not as *knowledge about*, but as *acquaintance with* the Creator and Sustainer of our lives. Accordingly he always, in prayer, employed the pronoun "Thou" in addressing Almighty God because he saw this as both the most intimate and the most reverent word in the language.

Seeing real prayer as the wrestling of the soul with God, Baillie's compositions for a month help those who are engaged in spiritual struggle. To encourage readers in their own efforts, he adopted the brilliant device of adding a blank page opposite each day's prayer, in order to give readers a chance to make their own personal contributions. Thus the book can be used as a devotional diary for the reader as it is for the writer.

After the sixty-two prayers for morning and evening of thirty-one days, Baillie adds two special prayers for Sunday. As I read these now, I am reminded of similar Sunday prayers produced by another famous Scot, Robert Louis Stevenson, who also combined rare sophistication with a truly childlike faith.

John Baillie was able to combine demanding public responsibilities with humility of spirit. He occupied a famous academic chair, conscious of a heritage of scholarship; he was professor of divinity in the University of Edinburgh and chaplain to the King; he was also dean of the faculty of divinity in Edinburgh and served a term as moderator of the General Assembly of the Church of Scotland, the highest office that the Church can bestow upon one of its members. Best of all, he never departed from the faith which nurtured him.

13
Thomas E. Jones

Tom Jones and I never had any real acquaintance until early September of 1945. At that time Tom was President of Fisk University in Nashville, Tennessee, and I was on the staff of Stanford University, California. We met at Richmond, Indiana, for the specific purpose of conferring on the prospect of joint service in Earlham College. With the war over and with the prospect of new life in the colleges, both of us thought seriously of new chapters in our lives. The Earlham Board was offering Dr. Thomas E. Jones the presidency of his *alma mater,* and he was inclined to accept the invitation; but, before making a final decision, he undertook to see what help he could get from potential colleagues. He understood that an increase in teaching staff would be required with the rise in student population, in the autumn of 1946, and he wanted to learn what the possibilities were before giving his final assent. Accordingly, he took the bus from Nashville to Richmond, in order to have a full day of conference.

We were drawn to each other at once, discovering that we had similar ideas about what a college ought to be and *could* be. Having already informed the President of Stanford University of my decision to vacate my post there, I was utterly free to discuss the future. Though I did not make a formal decision until after our return to Stanford for the autumn quarter, the conversation with Tom Jones was very nearly conclusive. After all, Tom was a very persuasive person.

The presidency of Tom Jones at Fisk University had already been a spectacular success. Starting from deep poverty when he began his tenure as President, Tom had built up a financial stability that was remarkable. He was influential in establishing the Negro College Fund and was successful in soliciting the financial support of influential donors who had never had an interest in Fisk before. Chief among these were Mr. and Mrs. John D. Rockefeller, Jr. The most fabulous of the Jones stories is that of visiting Mr. Rockefeller in his New York office, with no appointment, and inviting his new acquaintance to give the commencement address at Nashville. What is most remarkable is that Mr. Rockefeller, normally reticent about speaking, actually gave the address, and, as a consequence of the interest thereby aroused, contributed generously to University funds. It is doubted if anyone less persuasive than Tom Jones could have accomplished such a feat.

By the end of September 1945, Tom Jones and I had established a friendship which was an important part of the lives of both of us until the day he died. We did countless things together, the culmination coming on our joint work on his autobiography, *Light on the Horizon.* After his massive stroke in June 1972, Tom lay helpless in the Richmond Hospital for over two months, unable to say a word. Slowly I realized that the prospect of seeing the book was his fondest hope. Accordingly I arranged with the publisher to permit me to carry to the hospital some unbound pages. I placed the printed sheets of paper in my friend's left hand. He grasped the pages eagerly, smiled, and died the next day. In the crowded Earlham Meetinghouse, where we held the memorial service, more than thirty persons spoke.

From the beginning of our academic partnership, Dr. Jones made it clear that, though I was professor of philosophy, he expected me to do many things outside the classroom. Specifically he hoped that I could help him in recruiting teachers of both commitment and competence. Never jealous of his own authority as president, he wanted me to feel free to approach potential teachers wherever they might be found. He said that he trusted my judgment and I had good reason to be sure of his support.

The most vivid illustration of our new partnership came in April 1946, four months before my arrival at Earlham, when I met a man on shipboard who turned out to be Professor Landrum Bolling of Beloit College, Wisconsin. When Landrum asked why I was joining the teaching staff of a small college in Indiana I tried to tell him. Very soon he volunteered that if I were that much interested in the embodiment of a dream, he might be also. From England I wrote Tom Jones, who was still in Tennessee, telling him of the Bollings, of their plan of settling in Berlin for two years, and of the possibility that they might be persuaded to join the Earlham team. With no hesitation, Dr. Jones accepted my preposterous idea and wrote a letter of invitation to a man in Berlin whom he had never met.

The outcome of the Bolling episode was that Landrum later joined the Earlham team, first as professor of political science, then as general secretary for development, and finally as president. After his retirement from the presidency, Landrum Bolling became director of the Lilly Endowment and later chairman of the American Council on Foundations. If Tom Jones had not trusted me there is no reason to suppose that any of this would have occurred.

It pleased me that Tom Jones encouraged me to share in the burden of raising adequate funds to sustain the dream. The first important gift which came in this fashion was that provided by one of my Palo Alto friends, for the endowment of the Classics Department. A second happy experience, in the solicitation of funds, came by my connection with the Stout family, described in the final essay of this collection. The most exciting financial adventure of all was that involved in my long friendship with Eli Lilly.

Being in no sense a professional fund raiser, and having no formal training in that field, I was certainly a learner; but I had, in Tom Jones, the excellent advantage of a good teacher. What he taught me, both by precept and example, was that the donor should be offered a favor. Tom sincerely believed that a giver is fortunate in being able to share, however modestly, in what is already a going concern. He actually thought that Mr. Rockefeller was lucky in being able to invest in an institution as good as Fisk University. He thought that Eli Lilly was fortunate to be able to give added financial strength to a college already as strong as Earlham.

14
William Barclay

More than a million copies of the Daily Study Bible have been sold! This is a remarkable fact and one which tells us a great deal about its author, William Barclay. Though the death of this brilliant and devoted scholar has left a void because he wrote so much while he lived, we can go on learning from him for many years. *More than any other biblical scholar in our generation, William Barclay has shown that it is possible to be popular without being superficial and profound without being dull.* He did, indeed, combine the warm heart and the clear head.

My acquaintance with Professor Barclay was brief but valuable. I saw him in his own study at the University of Glasgow when he was the dean of the theological faculty of that venerable institution. One of my reasons for arranging the visit was to ascertain, for myself, whether there was any connection between him and the famous Quaker Barclays of the seventeenth century. I found that the two families are distinct, the apologist's family being limited to the eastern region of Scotland and William's family to the western area. It was obvious, as we conversed, that my question was a familiar one to the contemporary bearer of a great name.

As we talked, I mentioned the abundance of William Barclay's literary output. The total production from his pen is astounding! His answer to the question of how so much writing was possible was the simple one that he had the immense advantage of being deaf. His deafness, he explained, liberated him from the disturbing noises which harass most people and allowed him to concentrate on what he was doing, without interference or interruption. I could see that this was intended to be amusing, but I could also believe that it involved some seriousness. *Barclay looked upon noise pollution as one of the real miseries of contemporary life, which, by the simple act of turning off his hearing aid, could be avoided completely.* Often, as I have tried to concentrate in a motel room, with horrible noises beyond a thin wall, I have under-stood the Scottish scholar, and even envied him. In any case he did not complain about his obvious handicap.

We shall long remember William Barclay with gratitude because of his ability to bring clarity out of confusion in his introductions to the books of the New Testament. He combined knowledge of the Greek language with an unapologetic Christian commitment, which helped him to understand the New Testament authors who, long ago, shared this commitment. His understanding was, in part, a consequence of his firm belief. *The love of Jesus, he realized, is something which only his loved ones know.*

Valuable as Professor Barclay's New Testament studies are, his most permanent impact may have been made by his interpretation of the Apostles Creed. When there is a widespread tendency to look upon this ancient affirmation of the Christian faith as obsolete, Barclay is refreshing in his ability to make the items of faith sound both sensible and pertinent to our spiritual problems. Far from being contemptuous of the past, in the shallow conceit of mere contemporaneity, Barclay knew that wise early Christians had reasons, probably as good as ours, for affirming the faith by which they sought to live. This is why their words ought not to be lightly dismissed as though the authors were mere creatures of their time, without our supposed enlightenment.

What is obsolete, Barclay asks, *about believing that God really is and that he is personal? What is obsolete about recognizing that the clearest revelation of God's nature should be that of a Person, Jesus Christ?* The creed maintains that Christ died in reality, and not in some metaphorical sense, and that he rose in reality. *The creed makes it clear that a Christian must be part of a fellowship, including the total church of Christ and the "communion of saints" through the ages.* The creed employs the phrase "The resurrection of the body" to clarify the conviction that each person will have his own mark of individuality, though not that of the flesh as we know it. The people who claim that this is confusing, Barclay has taught us, are making a problem where none exists. What is irrational about the conception of a "spiritual body," which the New

Testament teaches? Of course it is not identical with anything we know in finite experience, but what valid objection can be raised to that? *In short, Barclay holds that there is no necessary contradiction between basic Christianity and sound common sense.*

Another enduring reason to remember William Barclay is his production of his life story, which in America is called A *Spiritual Autobiography.* This book, first published in 1975 under the title *Testament of Faith,* has helped many understand the roots of Barclay's powerful combination of faith and intelligence. The author does not minimize problems, as he has sought to be loyal both to his heritage and to the scientific mentality of modern men and women, but he is satisfied with the outcome. His very last sentence is memorable. He says, finally, that if he were "to begin life over again," he would "choose exactly the same service." Personally, I am glad that my own life has overlapped that of a person who has finished the course with such strong words.

15
Lowell Thomas

When I became eighty years old in December 1980, one of my prized letters was from Lowell Thomas. In the midst of this letter the famed communicator wrote, "Oh, to be eighty again." He lived on to August 1981, dying peacefully in his home on Quaker Hill, Pawling, New York, at the age of eighty-nine. At the time of his death he was, and had long been, the most eminent radio announcer of his country.

My friendship with Lowell Thomas came in 1944, when my wife and I visited him and sat in his studio while he made his evening news broadcast. What brought us together was a shared faith. It was his desire that I should give a sermon at the Quaker Hill Community Church, of which he was a strong supporter and leader. The old meetinghouse was still standing, but largely unused, and a new building to house the Community Church had been erected. Lowell wanted me to meet his neighbors, eminent among whom were Thomas E. Dewey and Norman Vincent Peale. It was appropriate that, when Lowell's memorial service was conducted at St. Bartholomew's Church in New York, his neighbor, Dr. Peale, provided the major address.

As the years went on, I was able to return to Quaker Hill and to balance the ledger by inviting my friend to Earlham as a speaker. He came in October 1965 and attracted the largest crowd ever known to have occupied Goddard Auditorium. As he spoke, one hundred fifty persons, mostly students, actually sat on the platform and on the steps leading to it. So tightly was the place packed that some of Lowell's hearers could touch his elbows as he spoke.

The people flocked to hear Lowell Thomas for many reasons. He had established his reputation as an explorer, a world traveler, a writer, and, above all, a purveyor of news by means of his own marvelous

68

voice. The voice was his finest asset, sometimes being compared to an organ. The deep, resonant tones were delightful to the listener. Millions learned to wait for the words with which he habitually concluded, "So long. . . . " The words became his trademark. Usually he added "until," but, in his final broadcast at the age of eighty-nine, he omitted any limitation. The change was amazingly prescient. In his letter to me last winter Lowell ended his letter in the familiar fashion, hoping for me another ten years.

Lowell Thomas never forgot that he was a son of the Ohio-Indiana border where he was born, in Darke County, Ohio, April 6, 1892. He sought to pay his debt to the area of his origin, this being one reason why he gladly accepted the invitation to speak at Earlham, where he refused any honorarium for his effort. His contributions to the cultural richness of Greenville, Ohio, will endure for many years.

The public reputation of Lowell Thomas was given its first major boost when he joined with T. E. Lawrence, "Lawrence of Arabia," in the final days of the First World War. The two young men met first in Jerusalem and appreciated one another at once. Lowell told me that, in only six weeks, he was able to acquire a working knowledge of the Arabic language. He made the friendship of several of the ancestors of the men who are today political leaders in the life of the Middle East. With the retreat of the Turkish army, the remaking of the map of the Middle East occurred speedily, and Lowell Thomas saw many of the changes at firsthand.

The times between the days with Lawrence and now have not been as exciting or as dangerous as were those at the end of the First World War, but no period, for more than a half century, has been dull. Always Lowell has had the knack of knowing where the action is. It is not surprising, therefore, that he has spent much time in Alaska.

We know a great deal about a person when we know who his heroes are. One of the outstanding heroes for Lowell Thomas was President Herbert Hoover. When I flew back from Saigon in October 1964 for the funeral of President Hoover at West Branch, Iowa, it pleased me to see Lowell Thomas in the vast assemblage gathered there. The fact that Herbert Hoover lived in New York City after the death of Mrs.

Hoover made it possible for the two friends to be together at will. Lowell realized keenly the unfairness of those public officials who sought to raise themselves by denigrating the reputation of Herbert Hoover and to blame him for what was really a worldwide economic disaster. He did everything he could to let the world know that President Hoover stood high in his estimation. This tells us something important about the character of Lowell Thomas himself.

III
Places

I am a part of all that I have met.

Alfred, Lord Tennyson

Starting from a very small community, I have had the privilege to know and love places far distant from the scene of my own origin. Now, living as I am in the last chapter of my life, I find that my memories of distant places are among the richest of those that I enjoy. Isolated in my own home, there is nothing to hinder my thinking of Cairo or Istanbul or Leningrad. Such places bring to mind the richness, not of one person, but of a multitude. In thinking of Leningrad, I go back to Peter and his magnificent dream of giving his beloved Russia an opening to the outside world. As I dwell on the founder of the city, I think of his enlarging experiences in Amsterdam and in London. Thus the contemplation of any one place leads, almost invariably, to other places, because their histories are intertwined. In the case of Istanbul, I am grateful again for the splendid course at Harvard in the history of architecture, which gave me my first understanding of the origins of the Byzantine style. And this contemplation leads me to Justinian and his remarkable career. Thoughts of Justinian lead me to Athens and the closing of the Academy. Once the mind dwells on Athens, there is seemingly no limit to the expansion of ideas. If I think of the Academy, with gratitude, as I do, I go on to think of Aristotle and of his Lyceum, of the Stoics, and so many more. Stoicism makes me think of Sir Gilbert Murray, possibly its best modern interpreter. I am glad that I once heard Professor Murray and enjoyed a slight connection with him. This makes me think of one of Murray's successors, also a visiting professor, T. S. Eliot, whom I had the privilege of hearing in Baltimore. This is how the mind works, particularly in old age, when there is abundant time to think and to remember. The usual procedure, so far as my own experience goes, is to start with places and to go on inevitably to the persons connected with those places.

Though our indebtedness to places is radically different from our indebtedness to persons, there is some overlapping. This is because the chief value of places arises from the persons who have enjoyed or developed local centers of culture. Our interest in Thermopylae, for instance, lies not primarily in the geography of the famous pass in Greece, but in the Spartans who died there. Our interest in a college derives not from its location so much as from the persons who have learned and taught there.

In my own life, the places which have influenced me are exceedingly numerous, so numerous, indeed, that I never begin to exhaust the possibilities of memory. And all of the connections are complex. Why did I have such a strong desire to visit the burial place of Cecil Rhodes, in the Matopos Hills, outside Bulawayo in Zimbabwe? The primary reason had to do, not with travel, but with the written word. In this case, my inspiration came from Olive Schreiner, whose *Story of an African Farm* I read almost sixty years ago. Reading her famous novel led to my reading her *Letters,* which led, finally, to a visit to the grandeur of the Matopos Hills, after a time at Victoria Falls. Without human connections the geographical scenes are never satisfactory. Victoria Falls is, indeed, one of the most awesome scenes on the planet; but, in my experience, the most moving sight of the area of the falls is the statue of David Livingstone. One intelligently compassionate person is worth a thousand falls, on the Zambesi or any other river.

Though it is only persons who represent intrinsic value, physical objects and locations may achieve instrumental value, provided they are viewed sacramentally. How physical objects may become sacramental is demonstrated by the old clock which is the centerpiece of my library. The clock affects me deeply, especially when I wind it every Tuesday and Saturday, knowing that my own father regularly used the same key when he wound it, starting ninety-two years ago. What moves me most is the thought of the labor which Father expended in order to be able to pay for the clock. How many bushels of corn did the twenty-three-year-old Sam Trueblood have to raise and sell in order to purchase an object by which my life is now dignified?

The fact that certain objects and places elicit deep emotion is not at all surprising, since we can experience a sense of reverence when thinking of:

> Ground where the grass had yielded to the steps
> Of generations of illustrious men.

Anyone who can visit the battlefield at Gettysburg, or the Lincoln Memorial in Washington, unmoved, is thereby revealing the superficiality of his own life. The words of Dr. Johnson, on the occasion of his visit to the island of Iona in 1773, have become the classic expression of this important theme. "Far from me and from my friends," he said, "be such frigid philosophy as may conduct us indifferent and unmoved over any ground which has been dignified by wisdom, bravery, or virtue. That man is little to be envied, whose patriotism would not gain force upon the plain of Marathon, or whose piety would not grow warmer among the ruins of Iona."

It is one mark of a great poet that he is able to evoke genuine emotion by reference to places otherwise unknown to the reader. I have never seen Tintern Abbey, but, thanks to William Wordsworth, I do not need to see it. Only a few people of the earth have visited Stoke Poges, but that does not keep Gray's "Elegy" from being the best-loved poem in the English language. The paradox is that a place becomes important when it preserves the memory of unimportant people. Personally I am moved when I repeat:

> Each in his narrow cell forever laid
> The rude forefathers of the hamlet sleep.

1
Waveland

Of all the places which I remember with gratitude, there is none that I remember more frequently and more affectionately than the place where I was born. My birthplace is a farm on the eastern edge of Warren County, Iowa, thirty-two miles southeast of Des Moines. My grandparents became settlers in what was called Waveland, early in 1869, arriving with five small children from their original home near Salem, Indiana. At Salem they were devoted members of the Blue River Quaker congregation that has produced many eminent Americans, including two presidents of Earlham College. Their Indiana farm was not far from the birthplace of John Hay, Assistant Secretary to President Lincoln and later Secretary of State. Coming from a community which included an academy, and which set great value upon education, Oliver and Mary Trueblood soon became involved in the building of another academy on the Iowa prairie, calling it Ackworth, after the name of the oldest Quaker school of England.

Each time I visit Iowa, I try to include some time in the cemetery where the bodies of my parents and others of my ancestors are buried. On each such visit I am vividly reminded of how hard the early days on the prairie were, with very little medical help in dealing with the inevitable crises of health. I am deeply moved when I see the first grave of the cemetery, that of my father's little brother, who died in the first summer of the new community, and whose grave determined the location of all subsequent ones. I realize that the cemetery determined the location of the first small meetinghouse, and of the subsequent one which was the scene of significant experiences in my own early childhood. I am always saddened when I see the graves of the five little Woodcock brothers. Summer after summer they died from maladies which would be curable now, for each hot summer on the prairie, with no refrigeration, brought its own sorrow. In one such summer my mother lost her first daughter, and her own mother, in the space of a few days.

As I stand reverently in the Iowa cemetery I realize that this is, indeed, the Heartland. Here is where segments of the westward march came together before being separated again on their way to the Pacific Ocean. The chief converging lines came from New England, Ohio, Indiana, and North Carolina. Most of us would never have existed at all apart from this convergence in the middle. The pioneers came partly because of the good land, which turned out to be even better than was supposed. In Hardin County some of the top soil is actually six feet deep.

The settlers in this richly endowed area tried to perpetuate their heritage by the use of place names. That is why we have Salem, Mount Pleasant, and New Providence. Because, until almost my own time, nearly everyone had come from some other place along the westward trek, a high point of each summer was the Old Settlers' Picnic. At first all were settlers since everybody was from somewhere else.

Remarkable as were the physical resources of the new communities, the spiritual resources were even more remarkable. The life which I experienced in my Iowa childhood did not seem to me at all unusual, but now I know that it was. It was unusual because of the almost perfect combination of the work ethic and high educational standards, united by Christian commitment. The work ethic was so strong that we never complained. We had no reason to complain because each one of us was needed if the agricultural venture was to succeed. I cannot remember, in my boyhood, sleeping beyond five o'clock any summer morning.

The educational standard which we took for granted owes more than is usually recognized to the powerful influence of William H. McGuffey. By means of his famous *Readers*, this man, almost single-handedly, made a lasting difference in the culture of the entire area. Even in my first schooling, we did not speak of grades, but always of *Readers*. When I began my formal education, McGuffey's name no longer appeared, except in the speller, but the new editors were faithful to a pattern of learning which had been established at Oxford, Ohio. The series which bears McGuffey's name actually sold, in only twenty years, sixty million copies.

By means of the *Readers*, we were made acquainted with many of the best literary productions of all times. In the *Fifth Reader* of my generation, for example, children were introduced to Milton's "Sonnet of His Blindness." We were as close to greatness as the written word could bring us. It was essential to this pattern of learning that much memorization occurred, it being expected that large sections of Shakespeare should be memorized and thereby retained.

The education and the work ethic went together perfectly. What better start than "A is for ax"? The natural sequence of the alphabet referred to the daily scene of each pupil's life. There was, of course, "box, cat, dog, nut, ox, pig, vine, wren, yoke." Why not? It is an obviously sound idea to combine common labor with the life of learning. McGuffey died in 1873, but the shadow he cast was still extended when I was born, as a child of the Heartland, in 1900. There was plenty of sin then, as there is now, but the pattern was priceless.

2
London

When the pursuit of my vocation began to require travel to various parts of the world, London was the first great city with which I became seriously acquainted. Now, after many subsequent visits, it still seems to me the greatest city in my experience. I come to this conclusion because of the way in which London arouses in me reminders of so many persons and so many movements which have contributed to the development of my own mind. I have often done my own writing near where Charles Dickens wrote *A Tale of Two Cities*. As I have written daily in the Library of Friends House I have tried to imagine the scene in its predecessor, Devonshire House, on the occasion there of the marriage of John Trueblood and Agnes Fisher, from whom I am descended. The two young Friends had met in London, John, it appears, having come to the great city from Lincolnshire and Agnes from Ulverston, near Swarthmore Hall. I try to imagine the excitement with which the young married couple arranged their departure from London to settle near the Carolina coast in 1682.

As I sit in the small garden off Aldersgate Street, north of St. Paul's Cathedral, I meditate on the remarkable experience which came to John Wesley in a building which once stood here, when on May 24, 1738, his life was literally turned around. As I lunch at the Cheshire Cheese, off Fleet Street, I can actually sit in the corner often occupied, first by Dr. Samuel Johnson and later, as the plaque on the wall tells us, by Charles Dickens. After lunch I can follow Johnson's steps to the preserved house nearby to express my gratitude in the very room in which the first adequate dictionary of the English language was produced. Still later I can walk quickly to the beautiful house of worship, St. Clement Danes, which is placed preposterously in the middle of the Strand. There it is my grateful privilege to sit in the north balcony where Johnson sat in order to be close enough to the pulpit to hear the sermon.

In Westminster Abbey I can sit in the Poet's Corner for hours, with no sense of boredom. I realize, as did T. S. Eliot, that the words of the dead are tongued with flame more than are the words of the living. At Bunhill Fields, one of the most inspiring burial grounds of the world, I can remember George Fox, John Bunyan, Isaac Watts, and Susanna Wesley. Across the street is the burial place of Susanna's most famous son.

At the Tower I remember how the young William Penn, while imprisoned there, wrote *No Cross No Crown*. When passing Newgate Prison, I remember how Elizabeth Fry instituted there a new way of looking at the lives of prisoners; at St. Paul's I remember Sir Christopher Wren and how he changed the skyline of the city after the Great Fire of 1666. Most moving is the Latin inscription, read by countless visitors to the majestic building, which may be translated as follows: "If you would see his monument, look about you."

One important occasion of my gratitude in London is the fact that, for several years, I was a member of the London Author's Club. Because it was known that my chairmanship of the Friends' World Committee would require both frequent visits and extended stays in the area, one of the members of the Author's Club presented my name and I was accepted. With a convenient location in Whitehall Court, near the Thames River, I found the facilities of the club well suited to my needs. I was grateful for a sleeping room, dining quarters, and library, in which I could, if I chose to do so, work for hours without interruption. Whitehall Court even provided sleeping accommodations for members of my family, if they accompanied me on one of my visits. I knew that London had long been famous for its excellent clubs, but the Author's Club provided me with my first experience of this highly civilized way of life. It was a special satisfaction on December 12, 1966, to celebrate my birthday at the Author's Club, supported by my London Friends. I almost felt like a Londoner! Again I thought of Johnson's words, "Sir, if a man is tired of London, he is tired of life."

Large as the population of London is, the daily working force is much larger. Some idea of this may be gathered from the fact that about ten thousand persons come every day from Brighton, sixty miles to the south. In one hour there are four trains, of twelve coaches each, traveling from Brighton to Victoria Station.

The public transportation of London is possibly the best in the world though the cost of this, like the cost of everything else, has increased. The three main constituents of public transportation are the double-deck bus, the taxicab, and the underground train. What is most delightful about the bus is the ease with which it may be boarded.

Contemporary London has its own problems and there will be others in the future, but there are areas in which its eminence is uncontested. It is still the safest big city of the world; it is the home of the most respected royal family in the world; it is the scene of the most brilliant public pageantry the world knows. I am grateful, personally, for the fact that some of my roots are on the north bank of the Thames.

3
Iona

Long before I first saw Iona, I was aware of its significance in Christian history. I was aware that the beautiful island of the Inner Hebrides, off the west coast of Scotland, represented an important step in the penetration of North Britain by the gospel of Christ. I admired Saint Columba (521-597) and felt sure that his method of evangelism could be given contemporary application, fourteen hundred years later. I naturally wanted to see, with my own eyes, where the famous saint landed in an open boat and where the Cathedral of the Isles had been reconstructed in the twentieth century. I wanted to share in the powerful fellowship which had been started in our time by George MacLeod, and to adopt, if I could, some of the spiritual discipline for which he is justly famous.

The first opportunity to visit Iona came in August 1948, in some free time between the sessions of London Yearly Meeting and the inauguration of the World Council of Churches at Amsterdam. It was my good fortune to be asked to give the Barclay Tercentenary Lecture at the former gathering and to represent Friends at the latter. Because London Yearly Meeting, in honor of Robert Barclay's Scottish birth, was held at Edinburgh that year, the extra distance to Iona did not seem to be an insurmountable barrier.

Three of us went together to the islands in 1948, my two valued companions being Howard Brinton and Thomas S. Brown. Since the experience was utterly new to all three of us, we faced it with keen anticipation, going by train to Oban and then by bus across the island of Mull. When we reached the western shore of Mull, we could see the great bulk of the cathedral across a narrow strip of water. It was as lovely in fact as it had been in expectation.

Our days at Iona, with George MacLeod and others, were creative for all of us. It is really doubtful if the Yokefellow Movement, with its own retreats, would ever have been established, apart from this 1948 experience. In a real sense, Iona is the "mother house." Like all members of the community, Howard, Tom, and I joined in worship, work, and study. We helped to carry the heavy beams to the roofs of the auxiliary buildings then being constructed, and Tom Brown made something of a stir by showing that he knew how to operate a string mop, thereby helping to keep the place clean.

The high moment spiritually came when there was, early Sunday, in the cathedral chancel, a celebration of holy communion. Because the experience was a surprise, we three Friends had no opportunity to discuss a common strategy. What was mildly surprising, therefore, was that each decided, on his own, to participate, for the excellent reason that to fail to do so would have been perceived by the others as sectarian exclusiveness or self-righteousness. Later, back in America, the two Philadelphia Friends were criticized by sectarians for their ecumenical spirit, but they were not disturbed by this because they had a good answer.

Having greatly profited from Iona in 1948, I was happy to introduce my wife to the scene in 1967, when, by good fortune, Lord MacLeod was present and was exceedingly hospitable. As we thought of the bravery of the early missionaries to Scotland, we were extremely grateful for the pattern which they demonstrated. They met on Iona for mutual strength, and then scattered to the mainland for service. When they were too tired, they assembled again for spiritual refreshment. Here is the basic Christian pattern of encounter and withdrawal.

The year 1979 was a critical time for Iona because the owner of the island, the Duke of Argyle, felt compelled to sell the land to meet his father's death duties. It was seriously feared that the historic island might be purchased by gambling interests or others almost equally damaging to the ancient image. Then came the good news, while we were in Britain, that the island had been purchased by the Fraser Trust and given to the nation. We can breathe a sign of relief because the image of Iona will not be lost.

4
Lake Paupac

Because it came into our lives when it was needed, I cannot think of Lake Paupac without a keen sense of gratitude. Lake Paupac lies in the heart of the Pocono Mountains of northeastern Pennsylvania, about thirty miles west of the Delaware River. The lake is a natural one, the overflow of which passes through two steep waterfalls as it descends Paupac Creek. Surrounding the lake, which is one mile long and a half-mile wide, is a large tract of forest land, most of which is still true wilderness, and in parts of which it is easy to get lost. Miles away from most of the signs of commercial confusion, the summer residents of the Paupac community feel a singular liberation from the noises and strains of ordinary twentieth-century existence. The sound of airplanes far overhead is sometimes the only reminder of scenes that are overbusy.

We purchased our share of the Paupac land in the autumn of 1949 and started construction of the writing studio in the summer of 1950. Our idea was to build the studio first and to follow with a residence later. The actual building of the residence took place in the summer of 1954. Both buildings are high above the water level of the lake and at about sixteen hundred feet above sea level. Cottages now surround the lake, but there is no unbroken road, the break coming at the inlet, a stream flowing from Promised Land. Like most of the earliest cottages, ours is located on the east side, providing stunning views of summer sunsets across the mountain water.

All of the studio construction was done by my sons and me, with the exception of the stone fireplace, built by a master mason. We found the stones we desired in a swamp on the west side and brought them up the hill on a sled. The studio has porches on two sides, the fireplace on a third, and a large window on the fourth, providing a resident writer with views of wilderness that are highly inspirational. We placed the large desk in the middle, so that I could see out whenever I paused in my writing. We made it a point not to install a telephone, since the value of uninterrupted writing was well understood. With good telephone service at the lodge, a half-mile to the south, we could be sure that we could be reached in any outside emergency. Each day, after completing my daily writing stint, I walked to the lodge to ascertain whether there were any urgent messages for any of us and to pick up the daily mail.

Since we were in Britain during the latter half of 1950, only a shell of the studio building was erected by my son Arnold that summer; but I was able to spend most of the summer of 1951 at Paupac and to help my son, so that the building was completed before Labor Day. We enjoyed the camp life as the summer progressed.

It gives me satisfaction now to remember the writing of nine books in the happy surroundings described above. All were written longhand on the big pine desk as I sat in the same Harvard chair which is now among the furnishings of Teague Library. It was part of my discipline to start writing each summer morning by eight o'clock, and never to write in the afternoon. The latter part of the day was spent normally in hiking, wood chopping, or sailing. In the evening I felt free to read or to examine what I had composed earlier in the day. I knew that the literary task had to be completed at Paupac because numerous duties at Earlham, after the beginning of the autumn term, would make sustained writing impossible. This is why the prefaces of several of my books are dated at Lake Paupac on Labor Day. The end of the season was sharp and clear.

The building of our Paupac residence in the summer of 1954 was a big event in our family life. The design of our house, consciously influenced by our life in California, was the joint work of Arnold and his mother. The central theme was that of making use of an outdoor living room or patio, with a stone ledge as its main wall. The plan turned out to be a pleasing one.

Our Paupac home now belongs to my oldest son Martin and his family. The scene has become increasingly delightful with the years, though it is no longer devoted to literary production as it was in the beginning. I like to remember productive days in the weather for which the Pocono Mountains are famous. I have been grateful for the opportunity to try to write in a setting conducive to literary production. The justification lies in the nature of the consequent effect on the lives of readers, most of whom I have never met, and whom I shall never meet.

The stimulation of the Paupac summer community was another thing for which I am permanently grateful. Each Sunday morning the summer residents gathered on the porch of Paupac Lodge to worship Almighty God and to express their support of one another. There were many dinners in the lodge with our neighbors, and times of sailing together were equally enjoyable. One beautiful dividend was the closeness of the friendships which developed among the children of neighbors. We were keenly aware of our good fortune and sought to be worthy of it by added efforts in service to the world outside.

My last major use of Paupac came in September 1966. I wanted to be away from the Earlham campus as college work began again without me. Because the neighbors left on Labor Day, I was almost entirely alone, and I loved the experience. Building big log fires and sitting before them, I spent most of the available time in meditation. Later in the autumn I was scheduled to speak in various parts of the country before going to Britain for an eight-month stay; but, in part of September, I was alone and had no duties. The experience provided a happy bridge between one chapter of my life and another.

5
Lake Mohonk

Lake Mohonk is one of the most beautiful of American communities. Located on a mountain ridge west of the Hudson River, at a latitude similar to that of Poughkeepsie, New York, it is, in one sense, a resort hotel, but, at the same time, it is much more.

On one side of the large hotel lies the sparkling spring-fed lake, while on the other is the Rondout Valley, across which can be seen the Catskill Mountains. The large surrounding woodland area is readily available by means of convenient footpaths, some of which are bordered by rustic pergolas designed for rest and meditation.

Albert K. Smiley, twin brother of Alfred, settled at Mohonk when the development of the area was minimal. His work was continued by Daniel Smiley, whose grandsons carry much of the responsibility today. Because there has been dedication to an idea in each generation since the beginning, unique features have been maintained. One is that, unlike nearly all other resort hotels, Mohonk has no bar room. Another is that, during the regular season, guests are invited, every morning, to participate in public worship. This experience, meaningful to several generations, includes the use of the organ, a hymn, Scripture, and prayer. On Sundays visiting pastors are invited to conduct full divine worship. Another rare and delightful feature is the absence of tobacco smoke from the dining room, which is maintained along with the requirement of decent attire at dinner time.

Outside the main building at Mohonk there are many operations which are both inspiring and educational. Scientific walks, stressing both botany and geology, are conducted regularly by resident scholars. Inside, seminars on scientific and philosophical topics are scheduled from time to time. A magnificent flower garden is maintained, with benches for the use of all who can profit from this particular form of healing ministry. Many, of course, engage in tennis, golf, horseback riding, and swimming; but others, glad to be away from urban stress, simply wander and think. The wanderer comes upon striking scenes, such as Cope's Lookout or Eagles' Nest. If he is thoughtful, he is also grateful for the many persons who, during more than a century, have helped to make all of this possible. The entire experience provides a deeper understanding of the meaning of the communion of saints.

My first experience of Mohonk occurred forty-seven years ago during a brief interlude between our life in Baltimore and that at Haverford College. Being only a visitor at that time, rather than a guest, I knew nothing of the story and was not personally acquainted with any of the Smileys. But later, when, as a member of the board of the Church Peace Union, I could stay several days, the beauty of the scene went deeply into my soul. I saw it as an embodiment of spiritual religion in a physical setting.

Most of my essays in this particular series have been devoted to individuals; but this one, by contrast, is devoted to a family. In late years, there has been no need of a single leader at Mohonk because standards have been maintained by group responsibility. Rachel, widow of Francis Smiley, plays the organ and helps to plan the excellent musical production provided by opera stars and members of symphony orchestras. Her son, Gerow, guides the outdoor staff, while her daughter, also named Rachel, assists her husband, Ben Mattison, the general manager of the operation. Ruth, wife of Keith Smiley, is the expert on flowers, while Keith travels widely and serves as chairman of the board. His brother, Daniel, keeps a close watch on natural resources, especially the water supply. Daniel's wife, Jane, manages the libraries.

My judgment is that we have not considered, adequately, the significance of family as a civilizing force. Each of us seeks, of course, to make a personal contribution, but individual lives are short and are soon forgotten. There is hope, however, if each generation can see itself as a part of an ongoing process, seeking thereby to make a difference in the world beyond what can be made by any individual working alone. There are several families in America which represent this operation magnificently, among them the Adams family, but we need a great many more. This is why the Smiley story is such an encouraging one. Albert K. Smiley pioneered well, but he did better than he knew. The chief reason for this happy result is that the pioneer builder has had successors who have understood loyalty to a dream as part of their Christian vocation.

6
Shakertown

My direct acquaintance with Shakertown began in January 1969, when I was conducting a teaching mission in a church on the south side of Lexington, Kentucky. To our surprise and delight, the congregation housed my wife and me in the Shaker Village, Pleasant Hill, south of the gorge of the Kentucky River.

We enjoyed the simple charm of the room which was assigned to us and to this same room we have returned many times on subsequent occasions. Since our introduction to the restored village we have, with the encouragement of the late Eli Lilly, tried to make good contemporary use of the old Shaker Meetinghouse. In this we have had the loyal assistance of professors and students of nearby Asbury Theological Seminary.

The Shaker Movement began with the development, in 1747, of radical convictions on the part of a few Quakers living in the North of England. Soon a leader emerged, in the person of Ann Lee, who declared that celibacy was a requirement of true spirituality. "Mother Ann," as she came to be called, arrived with six men and two women, in New York, August 16, 1774, and, after a stay of two years in the city, settled in the woods not far from Albany. By the time of her death in 1784, Mother Ann had recruited a band of followers and had formed "the United Society of Believers in Christ's Second Appearing." The prospect of the immediate end of the age made it relatively easy to persuade converts to abandon any hope of progeny.

The men and women, to whom was attached the nickname "Shakers," were formed into separated communistic societies, marked by devotion and hard work as well as generosity to strangers. Having no children of their own, they survived for over a century by conversions and by the adoption of orphans. Though strong societies were formed in New York and New England, the most prosperous Shaker community was that established at Pleasant Hill, Kentucky. This was, in part, a product of the Kentucky Revival of 1800-1802.

The Kentucky Shaker community prospered fabulously, as it engaged in an enlightened agriculture, stock breeding, and the production of some articles for sale in the outside world. All residents were assigned to "families" which included both men and women, living in strongly built houses which remain to this day. Central to all other features of the peaceful village on Pleasant Hill was the Meetinghouse in which worship was experienced with obvious enjoyment.

When the Pleasant Hill community ceased to exist in 1910, the buildings soon fell into decay; but, in our generation, there has been a successful restoration, providing a tourist attraction. Now, as a consequence of the devotion of Eli Lilly and many others, much of the land has been recovered and all of the chief buildings put in splendid repair. The dining room in the central building serves attractive meals, featuring Shaker dishes, graciously served by waitresses in Shaker dress. The family houses provide sleeping space for numerous guests.

What interests us now is the effort to make Shakertown something more than a mere museum. There were indeed good people who inhabited the community, and they flourished for more than a century; but now our concern is for the future. This we have tried to honor by the arrangement of conferences and retreats, some of which have had abiding effects upon the lives of the attenders. We find that people's ideas grow in an environment which includes a rare combination of simplicity and beauty. The Shaker furniture, which is elegantly simple, has an effect on the taste of the retreat attenders. The remembrance of generations of loving, self-effacing people, who combined work and prayer, is a lifting experience in itself.

We do not encourage the establishment of new societies on the Shaker pattern. For one thing, we think the practice of celibacy was a mistake. We think the ideal family size is that of five or six persons rather than seventy or eighty. But if we can be as devoted to an ideal as the Shakers were, we shall have reason to be grateful. Goodness is a rare quality, but the Shakers had it.

7
New Harmony

Though the main outlines of the New Harmony story had been known to me for a long time, my personal connection with the famous social experiment did not begin until the summer of 1967. I knew, in a general way, of the settlement of Rappites on the Wabash, early in the nineteenth century; I also knew of the purchase, a few years later, of the entire settlement by Robert Owen. I connected the Harmonists, in my own mind, with other Utopians, especially the Shakers and Amana Colonists; but I did not know much more.

My renewed interest in New Harmony came as an unexpected dividend from a visit to the island of Iona in June 1967. Having spent a little time on Iona in 1948, and having developed a friendship with Lord MacLeod, the leader of the Iona Fellowship, I desired to introduce my wife to the fabulous island and the reconstruction of the Iona Abbey.

Fortunately for us, George MacLeod was in residence at the Abbey when we arrived, and gave us ample time as we observed the embodiment of his dream of renewal. When, in the courtyard, we saw an unusual bronze figure, representing the Annunciation, our host shocked me by saying that I did not need to travel all the way to Scotland to see this, inasmuch as an exact copy existed in my own state of Indiana. When he said that the bronze figure was at New Harmony, occupying the central position in the "Roofless Church," I determined at once to visit the fabulous village and to see for myself. Learning that the vital connection was through Mrs. Kenneth Owen, wife of the great-grandson of Robert Owen, I secured her address and wrote to her before leaving Scotland.

On our arrival home, in the autumn of 1967, I received a letter from Jane Owen graciously inviting us to visit her at New Harmony. Mrs.

Owen, who divides her time between Houston and New Harmony, had already become the driving force in the restoration of the village.

On our first of several visits to New Harmony we were housed in the oldest of the reconstructed Rappite structures, next door to the excellent restaurant called the "Red Geranium." We were soon introduced to the interesting sights, including the communal buildings, the maze, the library, and the Harmonist Museum. What surprised us most was to learn that the ashes of the theologian Paul Tillich are buried in the village.

The initial success of New Harmony, 170 years ago, was amazing. Many of the followers of George Rapp were celibate, after the Shaker pattern, with the consequence that they gave themselves single-mindedly to the creation of a new kind of community. Having all things in common, the settlers believed that they were building a model of the kingdom of God on earth. The key to their success was unquestioning dedication to a particular dream. What self-interest could not have accomplished was made possible by deep commitment.

When it became obvious to Father Rapp that he and his followers were too far from other human habitations to have adequate markets for their products, he decided to sell the entire property and to go back up the Ohio River to the bend above Pittsburgh, to initiate another social experiment under more favorable economic conditions, the new settlement being called "Economy." Robert Owen, a wealthy industrialist of Glasgow, purchased New Harmony, determined to continue the experiment in communism. The new effort, however, soon failed, largely because many of the new settlers lacked the spiritual motivation which had appeared in the Rappites so strongly.

In our own generation, Lord and Lady MacLeod have come to Indiana from Scotland to participate in the dedication of the MacLeod "Barn-Abbey" established as a center of spiritual renewal for a large area, somewhat as the Abbey of Iona originally operated in Scotland. A new inn has been built to house visitors who share this vision, and retreats have been organized. The third chapter in the life of the New Harmony has begun.

IV
The Life of Learning

Gladly wolde he lerne, and gladly teche.

Geoffrey Chaucer

Because so much of my life has been spent in colleges and universities, it is not surprising that a great deal of my sense of gratitude should be centered upon academic institutions. There is a real mystique about colleges, enabling them to become objects of loyal devotion. The writing of my book *The Idea of a College,* unfortunately now out of print, gave me intense pleasure. It pleased me especially to think of colleges as pumping stations on the pipeline of civilization. I realized keenly that, since civilization does not maintain itself automatically, it can always decline. I saw also that civilization is bound to decline unless there are deliberate and sustained efforts to maintain standards. A college, I saw, is a fellowship which continues through generations for the purpose of producing the wisdom and virtue which no individual person can achieve alone. The unbroken heritage of learning and teaching is a particularly noble one.

My connection with colleges began early and has never ended. I grew up in the shadow of Simpson College and, even as a high school student, spent many hours in the Simpson Library, where I was always welcome. I have been a registered student in five institutions of higher learning and have taught in eight. The following essays give some indication of my academic Pilgrim's Progress.

My opportunities to know and to serve academic institutions have been widespread. Occasional lectures, sermons, and addresses have been delivered in more than three hundred colleges and universities. This number does not include addresses given in countries outside the

United States, some of the prized opportunities being in Great Britain and Hong Kong. From each such experience I have learned something which I might not otherwise have known. That is why I have employed the words of Chaucer as the epigraph of this section of the book. My careeer has had a variety of facets, but the central vocation has always been that of both learner and teacher.

As I look upon my life from the perspective of age I realize that many of my happiest times have been spent in the halls of Academia. I like to remember hours with Plato in Emerson Hall, Cambridge, and hours with other intellectual giants in John Hay Library, Providence. Though it did not occur to me in early years, I realize now that I have been very fortunate in my connections. Though I have worked hard, I gladly acknowledge that most of my blessings have been unearned.

One of the striking blessings of academic life is the opportunity it provides to be associated with stimulating associates. Recognizing this, I express my indebtedness to my own teachers, to my numerous colleagues, and to my far more numerous students. At every step of the journey I have been surrounded by people who know a great deal that I do not know, and who demonstrate skills which I do not possess. In nearly a decade on the Stanford campus, my closest friendships were formed with professors in departments sharply different from my own. Thus, I found myself frequently in contact with men of the sciences, particularly in the fields of physics and chemistry. I am thankful that it worked out this way. Academic people are fortunate, partly because they are always situated where they can be taught.

The emotional hold which American colleges have upon people who love them is an important feature of our culture and has led to generosity in giving, which is hard to match in any other culture. The general recognition of the intensity of college loyalty explains the almost universal response to a famous remark of Daniel Webster, "It is, as I have said, a small college, but there are those who love it." Webster was referring to Dartmouth, but his words can be applied to many other American institutions. No one who fails to appreciate the unique appeal of the American college can ever expect to understand civilization as it has developed between the Atlantic and Pacific.

Colleges have provided the main vehicle for my life's work because I have lived in them and worked in them for more than sixty years. Consequently college life is the life I know best. In each institution I have been filled with wonder as I have observed the way in which, with a complete turnover of participants, the reality of the fellowship can continue. Even though there is, in a few years, a total change in the fuel, the same fire goes on burning. It is, therefore, no accident that the most visible motto at Earlham College is the sentence taken from the log of the good ship *Woodhouse*, "they gathered sticks, and kindled a fire and left it burning." No man lives to himself alone and no man dies alone. It is thereby incumbent on anyone who has any understanding of the human situation to share his insights with any who are willing to listen and to learn all that he can from others. Intellectual vitality appears only in a fellowship, and it is such a fellowship that we denominate a college.

As I look lovingly at the books in my library, I realize that some of them which I most prize owe their origin to a fellowship rather than to the toil of a single individual. Sometimes this important fact is revealed in the printed dedication of a volume. A good example is that of *The Oxford Book of English Verse*, which I remove from the shelf more often than most. The brilliant editor, Sir Arthur Quiller-Couch, indicated his academic indebtedness by the following dedication:

To
The President
Fellows and Scholars
of
Trinity College Oxford
A House of Learning
Ancient Liberal Humane
And My Most Kindly Nurse.

Here is academic gratitude in the truly grand manner. In every case the awesome responsibility for the selection of "the best" from a period of six hundred years was that of the learned editor; yet he was aware that he owed the very standards, by which he judged, to the academic fellowship of which he was such a part.

It has been my privilege, during most of my long life, to live among persons upon whose minds I have been able to try out my ideas. In nearly every case the ideas have been altered by this operation. Ideas which are almost worthless in isolation thrive in the atmosphere of dialogue. This is why, as Lovejoy asserted, the history of philosophy is one long dialogic process. When ideas are challenged they may, thereby, be refined. In the nature of the case, Robinson Crusoe, even in DeFoe's fertile imagination, could not become a philosopher, so long as he was the sole resident of his island.

When I try to enumerate the persons to whom I am grateful, teachers come very high on the list. I realize, sorrowfully, that, so far as I know, every one of my many teachers is now dead. While I cannot, therefore, thank them in person, I can at least acknowledge them and express my gratitude by the written word. I hereby thank Ada Rogers, who taught me the importance of spelling, in a one-room school when I was eight years old. I thank my high school teachers, especially those in Latin and in English. I thank my professors in undergraduate and graduate education. Some of them gambled on me when I am sure I was a poor risk. It is part of wisdom about life to realize that, though we can seldom repay, we can always try to pass the torch to others.

1
The Speech Teacher

When I was fifteen years old, and a high school student, it occurred to my mother that she might employ someone to give me speech lessons. Though the idea was certainly unusual, this did not daunt her. "After all," she said, "we arrange lessons for piano playing. Why not do the same for the speaking voice?" Since we lived not far from Simpson College, it was not difficult to set up a regular schedule with the man who taught public speaking at the college, and who, I suppose, welcomed the small addition to his professor's salary. Certainly he took a genuine interest in his students.

Though the speech teacher has long gone to his reward, his generous use of time to help a young boy is still producing dividends. He was able to teach me the use of the diaphragm muscle to expel breath from the bottom rather than the top of the lungs. His conviction was that this simple process, which he compared to the action of a piston, is the chief secret of the production of an orotund quality in the human voice. Apart from his instruction, I doubt if I could have learned to place my voice so that the sound carries to a distance. The thin, weak voices, with which we are familiar, are not, said my teacher, necessary, but can be changed by attention.

The quality of public speaking which we encounter daily is, for the most part, remarkably poor. In spite of universal education, the majority of our people cannot speak well and cannot read aloud, except in a stumbling manner. It is really shameful that, after all of our expenditure of time and money on the support of public education, the majority of our people cannot say even a few sentences without the constant interpolation of the ugly sound "Uh."

There are many, today, who affirm that they were never taught oral reading. They seem to have no idea of how to employ pauses for the

105

sake of emphasis, twice as long after a period as after a comma. What is strange is that this is easily taught and need not consume any long time. Though almost anyone can be taught, in public speaking, to look down to get the text, and to look out to utter the words, there are few who follow this intelligent pattern. In reading the Scriptures, for example, the majority look down at the book during the entire time, thereby missing the beneficent eye contact between reader and listeners.

Since oral reading seems not to be taught in the schools, it may be necessary to teach it in the church. If I were a pastor, I should count it my privilege to try to give attention to the members who read the Scriptures before the congregation. That much of our Scripture reading in church becomes a meaningless ritual rather than something to reach lives is a terrible waste and one that could be avoided by deliberate attention.

Part of our decline is due to the fact that public speaking is no longer emphasized in colleges and universities. Once it was assumed that an educated person could be counted upon to demonstrate excellence in the spoken word, but that is true no longer. Once the colleges took great pride in debating and in extempore speaking contests, but today there are colleges in which this is not even a part of academic life. Fortunately, my own alma mater, William Penn College, has decided to be nonconformist and to require participation in debate on the part of all members of the academic community.

In my own career, I owe a great deal to the fact that I engaged in debate in both high school and college. Preparation for the debates drove me to the public library. As I think of hundreds of hours there, I am even more grateful for Andrew Carnegie, who provided the library building in our town, as in so many other communities. I never saw Mr. Carnegie in the flesh, but I thank God for his generosity. When I go back now to Indianola, Iowa, I usually make it a point to enter the Carnegie Library and relive some of the happy hours spent there sixty-five years ago.

2
William Penn College

When I completed my studies at the public high school in Indianola, Iowa, I quickly realized, that, being only sixteen years old, I was too young to enter college. There was never any question in my mind, or in the minds of my parents, whether I would go to college, but timing was important. Because I needed time to grow and to earn a little money I stayed out of formal education for a full year. This is a decision for which I have long been grateful. As much as I could, I earned money by hiring out to other farmers in the community. For working twelve hours a day in harvesttime I was able to earn, besides room and board, $37.50 a month, and to save nearly all of it for future college expenses. Since I was not yet fully grown, it was difficult to keep pace with big, strong men in shoveling wheat, but somehow I was able to do it. Possibly the strongest motive was pride. When there was no farmwork to do, either at home or for neighbors, I read books which my high school education had brought to my attention and wrote frequently in a notebook. I was enjoying time to grow both physically and mentally.

In September 1918 I enrolled as a freshman at Penn College, the Quaker college situated at Oskaloosa, Iowa, sixty miles southeast of Des Moines and near the Des Moines River. Since the World War was still raging, the number of male students was small, and the total enrollment was only about two hundred. The Quaker influence was strong, most of the students having come from backgrounds similar to my own. Being only seventeen, I was not yet subject to the military draft, and never became subject to it because the war ended before my eighteenth birthday.

Though, during my freshman year at Penn, the male students were too few to make possible collegiate football, this situation was radically altered at the beginning of my sophomore year. Accordingly I tried out for football and found real profit in the sport. At first I was an absolute beginner, never having had the opportunity to engage in organized sports in high school because of farm chores. I loved college football, partly because I prized the experience of being tested to the limit of my powers. The man opposite whom I often played in practice weighed nearly three hundred pounds. It was good for me to learn that it is possible to continue, when all nature cries out to stop. It pleased me to win football letters in both my junior and senior years.

Not as much philosophy was offered as I desired, but I rejoiced in being provided excellent instruction in both history and English literature. The fact that, as a freshman, I was required to submit a six-hundred-word essay every Monday morning provided a discipline for which I have been grateful ever since. How my composition teacher, Anna Eves, could take amateurish papers seriously I do not know, but somehow she survived. She is high on my list of persons to visit in heaven. Fortunately, in college, I was encouraged by several instructors to memorize long passages, especially of poetry. These passages constitute a valued resource to this day.

There was nothing the Penn College of my day stressed more than public discourse. By a splendid turn of the wheel, a similar emphasis is being made at my alma mater at this time, largely because of the vision of President Turbeville. In 1918 and the years immediately following our little college stressed debate and excelled in intercollegiate contests of this character. Soon we were expected to think on our feet and to speak wholly without notes. In my senior year at Penn, I was privileged to represent the college in the State of Iowa Extempore Speaking Contest, in which we received first place. I was given a gold medal, but I do not know where it is now.

As I look back, after the lapse of sixty years, it is my sober judgment that the little Quaker college in southeast Iowa provided me an excellent preparation for my public career. We were sufficiently small for each one to be needed and to be recognized as a person, but we had sufficient strength to provide what Whitehead later called the "vision of greatness." Whenever I could, I spent time alone in the stacks of the college library, which, though not large by some standards, were large enough to include the greatest books ever written. The balance between football, debate, reading, and a simple social life was what a boy from Warren County, Iowa, needed. Of course we never traveled outside the state, and there was really no need to do so. In fact, I was never outside the state until I graduated from college and went at once to New England. Speakers came to us from far away, and we sought to learn as much from them as they were willing to impart. Whenever possible I took advantage of the invitation given by visiting speakers to meet with them personally. Thus a genuine contact with the big world was maintained.

The important thing about Penn College sixty years ago was its vision of wholeness. I do not remember any suggestion of the necessity of having to choose between intellectual integrity and spiritual vitality. We did not have an athletic sector, segregated from the remainder of the academic community. The same young men played football and debated and participated in the Student Volunteer Movement, intending to engage in mission work of some kind. It is not really surprising, therefore, that a very high proportion of the young men and women who were Penn students sixty years ago became leaders in many different walks of life. They achieved leadership partly because this was what their elders and their peers expected of them. The little college, sixty years ago, did not have much money, and it had very little prestige; but it had a unique power, the power of *expectancy*.

3
Brown University

In February 1923 I faced a really difficult decision. Being only twenty-two years old, and never having been outside the United States, I was given the tempting offer of a teaching position in Shanghai. The appeal of a distant post was great, but the reasons for declining the invitation were also great.

The invitation came in the office of W. H. P. Faunce, the distinguished President of Brown University, in Providence, Rhode Island, in which I was then a graduate student. President Faunce came quickly to the point: I was being asked to become the representative of "Brown in China," with the responsibility of teaching in Shanghai University and financial support provided by Brown in the United States.

Enticing as the surprise offer was, I soon decided to decline it, chiefly on the grounds that I needed more training before venturing on such a difficult task. In consequence of my refusal I went on to study at Hartford Seminary for a year under the tutelage of Alexander C. Purdy and for two years at Harvard, where my chief guidance was that of Willard L. Sperry. Though I have never regretted the decision, I have often contemplated the difference that acceptance would have made in my life.

President Faunce was an impressive person to meet. Closely connected with persons of influence in the nation, especially John D. Rockefeller, Jr., he guided Brown through one of its most successful periods. What impressed me permanently in our interview was his long silence. After telling me the surprising purpose of our conversation, the president suddenly stopped talking, took a notebook from his coat pocket, and began to write. Not able to know the reason for the interruption, I simply waited silently until he finished writing and had returned the notebook to his pocket. Then he said, "I hope you can forgive me for this seeming discourtesy of stopping our conversation. The reason for the interruption is that, suddenly, I had an idea, and I learned long ago that I have to put down ideas when they come, if I do not wish to lose them." Immediately I said that I was immensely grateful for the opportunity of observing a practice which I hoped I could adopt in my own life.

I did not go to Shanghai and I have never been in Mainland China, but I have thought countless times of Dr. Faunce with real gratitude because he gave me something which otherwise I might have missed. For years I have tried to follow faithfully the practice of putting ideas on paper as soon as they occur. Like Dr. Faunce, I soon learned that failure to record at once often entails permanent loss. Consequently my library contains far more of my unpublished than of my published thoughts. Ideas, by being faithfully recorded, tend to grow, often producing fruits after long periods of quiet culture. Ideas are, indeed, my capital.

How can a person make repayment for a personal debt? Obviously it is seldom possible to repay the donor, for he may be gone. My professors at Brown, along with the president, have all passed to their rewards. I am thankful to them for their confidence in a young man whose experience was certainly meager, but I cannot express my gratitude to them now. What I can do, and what I have done, is to pass on the fruitful ideas to younger generations, especially those of my own students. To many of these at Guilford, Haverford, Stanford, Harvard, Earlham, and Mount Holyoke I have said repeatedly, and often humorously, "Put it down," "Do it now." These three-word advices have been taken seriously by a good many women and men, and thereby my debt to President Faunce has been partially repaid. I hope that, in heaven, he is laughing about this right now. Perhaps he still has a notebook in which to record such ideas.

As I have looked back on that decisive interview in 1923, I have often wondered what it was that Dr. Faunce was writing. I never asked him, for that was none of my business. My guess is that what he wrote had nothing to do with our particular interview. The likelihood is that the thoughts recorded were entirely extraneous. My reason for believing this is that I find this is how my own mind works. Ideas come in a flash, usually with no immediate connection with what is transpiring at the moment. I have learned to stop all else, if this is possible, and do the recording before it is too late. Sometimes this means stopping the car I am driving, parking it by the side of the road, and writing for a few minutes. When a really appealing idea enters my consciousness in the night, I find it wise to rise from my bed and to put it down. If not, it may be gone by morning.

The thoughtful reader of this essay will quickly realize that the Faunce practice is only possible if pen and paper are available. Many people lose ideas forever because they have not followed the practice of providing themselves with recording materials. A golden text for the would-be thinker becomes, therefore, "You also must be ready," Luke 12:40 (RSV).

4
Harvard University

When, in the autumn of 1924, I enrolled in Harvard University, there were many reasons for my decision. Among them was the wide range of choice in studies which Harvard made available. The payment of tuition in the divinity school enabled me to profit by courses in any of the university departments, at the graduate level. Accordingly, I soon participated in courses in English literature and in philosophy. Among courses valuable to me to this day were Seventeenth-Century Religious Literature, Thomas Carlyle, Poetics, the History of Gothic Architecture, and the Philosophy of Hegel. Such studies supplemented my theological studies in a satisfactory way.

Another important reason for seeking to study at Harvard was the admiration I already felt for the dean of the divinity school, Willard L. Sperry. I admired him both as a speaker and as a writer and was aware of the high standard he required of his students. As soon as I could do so, I arranged to write for him a paper each week, expecting and receiving his critical comments. There was ample evidence that he had read each paper carefully and for this I was grateful. Soon he suggested that I go through, with him, the two long poems of Wordsworth, The Prelude and The Excursion, making notes and engaging in subsequent dialogue. This effort differed from anything I had experienced in my academic life up to that time. I began to understand what it meant to experience "emotion recollected in tranquility."

Sperry's practice of tutorial teaching, with one student guided by one instructor, was a result of his experience at Oxford University, where he had the privilege of being a Rhodes Scholar. The experience which he graciously introduced into my life was in sharp contrast to the mass teaching, so common today, in which there is no personal contact at all.

The chief course taught by Dean Sperry was that in the Art of Preaching. To have a person of his character in my congregation as I engaged in my amateurish efforts in the Andover Chapel meant that I undertook my task with what Sperry always called "high seriousness."

Nine years after taking the theological degree at Harvard there came to me the gratifying invitation to take Dean Sperry's place for the summer of 1935, as acting dean of the Harvard chapel. My chief responsibility was that of conducting worship each morning, Monday through Friday, in the splendid building at the heart of the Harvard Yard. The student attendance was good and continuing friendships were made. One by-product, which I did not envisage in advance, was the opportunity to write my first book for publication, writing every word on Dean Sperry's desk in Memorial Church. Most of the chapters in this book, entitled *The Essence of Spiritual Religion,* were enlargements of the brief talks given in daily chapel. My method, which I have followed since that time, was to speak without notes and then to write afterward as soon as possible, while the ideas were fresh in my mind. Of particular satisfaction to me, in the summer of 1935, was the fact that my sons, Martin and Arnold, aged ten and five, were nearly always present, mingling with the college students. This was possible because we lived nearby in the home of Professor Henry J. Cadbury.

Another happy connection with Dean Sperry came in the autumn of 1944, when I was enjoying a partial sabbatical leave from Stanford University, with the family established in the attractive village of Newtown, Connecticut. Since it was wartime, automobile transportation was difficult, but I could reach Boston and Cambridge each Sunday evening by taking the train from New Haven. My academic task at Harvard was that of teaching the Philosophy of Religion. In doing this I followed, in large part, the development of ideas already published in the book *The Logic of Belief.* Again I made friendships, some of which have survived. For my living quarters four days each week I was given the use of a suite in Lowell House, where I also took my meals. By this arrangement, I was able to experience firsthand the

House plan initiated by President Lowell. It was an enlarging experience.

As I look back, I realize that all three of my Harvard periods have affected my life deeply. Among my fondest memories are those of walking through the famous yard and thinking of persons in other generations who had walked over the very same ground. To sit in Divinity Chapel and to remind myself that I was sitting where Ralph Waldo Emerson sat was an experience that I never took lightly. Harvard did many things for me, but the best of all is that it made me begin to understand what it means to be surrounded by a cloud of witnesses. It was at Cambridge that I first tried to take seriously the communion of saints.

Now all of the saints who influenced me fifty-five years ago are gone. I cannot listen now to George Foot Moore, Willard L. Sperry, William Ernest Hocking, Henry J. Cadbury, or Bliss Perry. But there is one thing I can do. I can remember.

5
Guilford College

The memories of Guilford College are precious ones, partly because the Guilford appointment was the first of my teaching career. When, working in Cambridge, Massachusetts, in the late spring of 1926, I received a letter from President Raymond Binford, I was highly pleased. The invitation helped me to decide the nature of my ministry in the world. President Binford asked me to teach the philosophy courses and to be Dean of Men. The prospect was exciting on both counts.

We moved to the Guilford campus in September 1927, occupying a house then located near Founders Hall. Thus we were in the middle of the operation. My office was in Cox Hall, the chief dormitory for men students, and our living room was filled every Sunday night by those who attended a campus Christian fellowship.

For the first time, I undertook to teach a course in Christian Classics, modeled on the course Dean Sperry had offered at Harvard. It was a delight to see how eagerly the young men and women from the farms and towns of North Carolina accepted the challenge of the ideas of such people as St. Augustine, Thomas à Kempis, and Blaise Pascal. The way in which the written word transcends both time and space filled my mind with a sense of wonder. It was then that I began to think of the "habitual vision of greatness."

More than fifty years ago our life at Guilford College was in full swing. The college was a good place in which to live and work, limited to only a few hundred students and served by a highly dedicated staff under the leadership of Raymond Binford as President. All of us watched expenses very carefully, my own salary amounting to $2,750 a year, out of which we paid rent for our campus home. If I traveled anywhere I had to pay for it myself, while for hospital and medical

116

bills there was no insurance. On the other hand, we paid no income tax and no tax on property since we had none.

As I look back now, I am sincerely grateful for my life at Guilford. The campus scene with two halls for women, and two for men, was essentially peaceful. There were naturally some problems as there always are when persons are involved, but they were manageable ones. As dean of men I knew all the men students and most of the women; and, as professor of philosophy, I personally taught a large proportion of the students. When I meet some of those same people now, they seem like contemporaries, but then I thought of them as young persons. One of them, Joseph Cox, is now retired and lives in Friends Homes, adjacent to the Guilford campus. Every time I visit North Carolina I meet some of these good friends for whom I was responsible from 1927 to 1930.

It is hard for modern collegians to know how close-knit the campus life of fifty years ago really was. Those of us who did the teaching visited the home communities from which our students came, talked to their parents, and shared their dreams of the future. We were concerned with proposed marriages, with possible graduate study, with problems of faith, and with professional careers. We rejected entirely the idea, later to be popularized, that professors should limit their work to the classroom. We believed and practiced the philosophy of wholeness.

It is important to realize the degree to which the women and men who taught at Guilford felt that they were members of a team rather than mere employees. We cared about the little college, and when the great depression crisis came, we voluntarily shared the burden. In January 1930, when it was evident to all that the crisis was real, we decided to cut our meager salaries in half. How we made it, I hardly know; but somehow we survived, even though, by that time, our second son had been born.

Guilford College, when we lived there, was a rural scene, six miles out the Friendly Road from the city of Greensboro. Our milk was processed by students on the campus and a large proportion of the young men and women worked for board and room, performing janitorial and dining room tasks. Several young men cared for the farm animals. It seems like an impossible dream now, but it really existed, and it was good. Though I have served, in subsequent years, in situations vastly different, I shall ever be grateful that my first teaching experience occurred at the Quaker college of what still seems to me the most beautiful state of the Union.

6
Johns Hopkins University

My decision to begin philosophical studies at Johns Hopkins University was one of the major decisions of my life. My registration occurred in September 1930, less than a year after the beginning of the Great Depression. With my wife, Pauline, and my two young sons I settled happily in a house on the northern edge of Baltimore, the elder son, Martin, enrolling in the Friends School. Each morning I delivered my son to the school on North Charles Street and drove to the Homewood Meetinghouse where I had an office. Each day was occupied with work in the office across the street from the Homewood campus of the university and in attendance at seminars or in study in the university library. There I was assigned a cubicle, in the stacks, where I could keep the books I was using without the burden of returning them constantly to the proper shelves.

Though I had no firsthand acquaintance with Johns Hopkins prior to 1930, I had long admired the institution, conscious of its pioneer role in graduate study on the German model. I was glad to join, in a modest fashion, in a heritage which had shaped the academic standards of such scholars as Woodrow Wilson and Josiah Royce. I soon saw that if I were ever to earn the Ph.D., I should have to make all of the major moves myself. Though Professor Arthur O. Lovejoy became at once the guide of my thinking and writing, he made no move regarding requirements. It was strictly up to me to determine when I should sit for the qualifying examinations in the German and French languages, and to arrange for the general examinations which came later. I knew that few persons had been awarded the degree under Professor Lovejoy's stern leadership, but I was determined to complete what I had begun. The degree was awarded in June 1934.

The combination of circumstances which enabled me to pursue

graduate studies at Johns Hopkins was fortunate. I could not have started on the course apart from the generosity of Baltimore Friends, who appointed me their executive secretary at Homewood. The modest salary connected with this appointment provided support for our little family and made possible payment of tuition charges. The payment to the university was cut in half because of my work in organizing and sustaining a luncheon club on campus. The club, made up of young men who met with me once a week, came to be known as "The How To Be Religious Although Intellectual on Wednesday Club." One remarkable consequence of this fellowship was that, with some of the members, it has continued to this day, both in correspondence and in personal contact. Some of the men went on to theological seminaries when they left Hopkins. Because the officers of the university seemed glad to have a movement of this character in existence among them, they encouraged it.

Another valuable fellowship of those depression days was the gathering of young people every Sunday evening in the Homewood meetinghouse. Very early they appreciated the connection, for they could see a portrait of Johns Hopkins, the founder, near where their meetings were held. The portrait was there because the founder had formerly been a member. It was in these Sunday evening meetings of young people at Homewood that we began the emphasis, continued ever since, on the ministry of common life. It meant a great deal for a physician from the famous Johns Hopkins Hospital to try to tell students what the sources of strength in his life really were. *We liked to ask, "What, in your life, has been the greatest reward?"*

My connection with Professor Arthur O. Lovejoy was twofold. On the one side it involved participation in his famous seminars, most of which had to do with the history of ideas. I was especially helped by an entire semester devoted to the right and the good. We sat around a large table in King Hall with Lovejoy at the end. With his iron-gray hair erect in a crew cut, he always seemed German in appearance, his studies in Germany, as a young man, having set the tone of his scholarship. Never marrying, his devotion to the scholarly career was unusually single-minded.

The other connection with my mentor was that of my visits to him alone in his apartment on Park Avenue. The procedure was that I should write an essay, send it to him by mail, and then visit him about a week later. The purpose of each visit was to learn all that I could from his criticism. Fortunately, he was as ruthless as he was courteous, forcing me to defend every conclusion I made. *Always the questions were the same: "Is it true? Does it follow? Can you think of any exceptions?"*

The choice of a dissertation topic was very important, for the earning of a degree depended upon the quality of the actual production, which was meant to add to the sum of knowledge. At first I considered the moral philosophy of Albert Schweitzer and actually wrote to the great man in Lambarene, West Africa. Though Schweitzer replied, graciously supporting my project, I soon abandoned the idea because, under Lovejoy's influence, I had fastened upon another theme. The topic chosen, early in my Hopkins career, was in the field of philosophical anthropology and was finally termed "The Differentiae of Man." *I had come to see that the most important fact which we know about our universe is that, at one point, it has persons in it.* Without conscious intent, I had become a philosophical personalist, and I wished to learn, as much as is possible, what a "person" is. Professor Lovejoy encouraged this line of study, partly because it was congenial to his own thinking. The dissertation, which I defended before a distinguished company of scholars, now sits on a shelf in my own study, but it has never been published in full form. Nevertheless, the ideas in it have appeared, in various forms, in my published books.

7
Haverford College

In the late spring of 1933, as I sat in the office of Baltimore Yearly Meeting, I received a letter from Rufus Jones, which was destined to make a radical change in our lives. The letter said that, for two reasons, Haverford College expected to add to the staff of the department of philosophy. The first reason was that Douglas Steere planned to be in Europe during the academic term, 1933-34. The second reason was that Rufus Jones, himself nearing the age of seventy, envisaged retirement at the end of the teaching year. Haverford, said Dr. Jones, needed a person who could, for one year, teach the courses previously taught by Douglas Steere, and also one who might be expected to take over, later, some of the courses long taught by Professor Jones. Dr. Jones invited me to spend a day on the Haverford campus, during which time he believed a decision could be made.

The day of my Haverford visit was a Thursday, deliberately chosen because it was the day marked by public worship in the Haverford meetinghouse. Fifth Day meeting was then attended by all of the students and by nearly all of the professors. I was pleased to contemplate being part of a college which could maintain a heritage of such worth.

During the day I met with President William W. Comfort, as well as with Douglas Steere and Rufus Jones and a few other professors. The hours in the study of Professor Jones, on the second floor of his campus home, were especially valuable. We talked of the course in ethics required of every Haverford senior, without which graduation from the college was impossible. The good man said that, if it were decided that I should join the Haverford faculty, he wanted me to help in this course, which he expected to teach for the last time in the autumn of

1933. It was also suggested that, in the seminar for senior majors in philosophy, we should share the responsibility equally, the first semester being devoted to Kant and the second to Hegel. The seminar was always conducted in the home of Rufus and Elizabeth Jones, which faced the cricket field. As I left the Haverford campus for my return to Baltimore, President Comfort said that I was invited to join the faculty and I accepted at once.

We moved to Pennsylvania in September 1933, and soon I was deeply involved in the most strenuous year of my life. I taught three courses each semester and also wrote, each month, a full chapter on my Hopkins dissertation. For the consideration of the dissertation I went by train at the end of each month to meet with Professor Lovejoy at his home in Baltimore. It was a hard year, but a happy one; and it ended in June 1934 with the award of the Doctor of Philosophy degree from Johns Hopkins University.

My three years at Haverford were rich in new friendships, including that of President Comfort and a remarkable elderly man, J. Henry Bartlett, whose very presence adorned the Haverford Meeting on both Sunday and Thursday mornings. Recognizing no generation gap, I prized the connections with older persons who had so much to teach me. One of these was Amelia Gummere, whose splendid Rancocas edition of the *Journal of John Woolman* had already made her the foremost Woolman authority. Today in my library are some books which once belonged to this brilliant woman.

The most unexpected development of my three years at Haverford was my appointment, first as associate editor, and then as editor, of *The Friend*. With my doctoral dissertation behind me, I had time for other writing; and, more and more, this appeared in the pages of *The Friend*. My teaching duties during my second and third years at Haverford were such that I could spend one day a week in the office of the magazine, 304 Arch Street, Philadelphia, the actual writing being done in my home. Richard Wood performed the important task of editorial management, thus setting me free to write. The production of an editorial every two weeks for several years was an experience for which I am exceedingly grateful. The regular writing prepared me for the toil which was later to be required in the production of publishable books.

8
Stanford University

Though I had known of Stanford University by reputation nearly all of my life, my first personal connection with the noble institution did not occur until my thirty-fifth birthday. On that day there came to me at Haverford College, where I was teaching philosophy, an invitation from Ray Lyman Wilbur, President of Stanford University, to meet him in a Philadelphia hotel. Not knowing what to expect, and never having met Dr. Wilbur, I faced the interview with puzzlement. Already I knew that Dr. Wilbur had been Secretary of the Interior in President Hoover's cabinet, as well as president of the university. I soon found that, like many important men, he was personally friendly. Ray Lyman Wilbur, a tall Lincolnesque man, I found easy to meet. Later our connection ripened into a genuine friendship, so that he treated me almost as one of his sons. The connection with the Wilbur family became finally so close that our son Arnold stayed with the Blake Wilburs while we went abroad; and, on two different occasions, we took the Wilbur grandsons to Britain with us. But, on that December day in Philadelphia, all of the personal aspect was still in the future, and the good man came right to the point. A position at Stanford, he said, would be open in June 1936, and he wanted me to consider it. Because Harvard men, earlier in the week, had recommended me, he suggested that I visit Palo Alto in the break between semesters. Since there were no good facilities for flying, it was decided that I should travel by the Overland Limited at the end of January, give one sermon in the Stanford Memorial Church, and meet some of Dr. Wilbur's senior advisors. The proposed train journey was, of course, longer than any I had ever taken in America, and I faced it with keen anticipation. I had never previously been farther west than Nebraska, and the prospect of a ride through the Rocky Mountains was exciting.

On Sunday, in the famous chapel, I did the best of which I was capable, presenting the case for spiritual religion, in contrast to its many alternatives. There were splendid opportunities to meet with the elder academic statesmen and their wives at the president's house on the campus. The outcome was that, as I departed, Dr. Wilbur offered me the position of chaplain of the university and professor of the philosophy of religion. I had already told him that, being concerned equally for the practical and the intellectual, I could not accept any invitation that did not include both aspects of my career.

Pauline met me in Philadelphia as I arrived from California and, after learning the details of the Stanford offer, agreed that it should be accepted. Accordingly, I dispatched a telegram to Dr. Wilbur, and our future was, for a few years, settled. It was not easy to tear up our safe roots at Haverford, which included the editorship of *The Friend*, but we both decided that the bold thing was the right thing. We never regretted this decision.

As soon as my Haverford duties were completed, in June 1936, we drove across the continent with our two young sons, Martin and Arnold, then aged ten and six. Having arranged to purchase a home on the Stanford campus, we soon settled into what was, in many ways, an idyllic way of life.

Part of the joy of our new life on the Stanford campus was my first serious attempt at gardening, especially in the nurture of flowers. This was something for which I had never had either time or space before. Because of the mild climate at Stanford I was able to raise flowers hitherto unfamiliar to me. Another attractive aspect of our new scene was the proximity to the campus school, where our young sons were very happy in both studies and games.

At 747 Delores Street, we were surrounded by professors' families and fraternity houses. Some of the professors were men of national reputation, but this did not hinder the development of close friend-ships which endure to the present day. The most famous of our close neighbors were the Hoovers, whom we saw almost every day on their walks. The house near us, then owned by President and Mrs. Hoover, was, after her death, given to the university and now serves as the president's house.

Part of the attraction of the dual position at Stanford was that it provided me, for the first time in my life, with a full-time secretary who was able to take dictation and also to produce excellent typed copies of anything I decided to write. I soon saw that at Stanford I had a splendid opportunity to write journal articles, essays, and books for publication. Having already produced one book at Harvard in the summer of 1935, I realized that I could produce more if only I could arrange my time for such a purpose. The secret, I soon discovered, was that of living my life in chapters. I remembered the amusing response of Rufus Jones to the student who asked him when he had time to write so many books. "On Tuesdays" was the laconic reply.

The position at Stanford opened to me a large opportunity to meet powerful minds, whom I might never have encountered otherwise. As chairman of a lecture committee, I acted as host to a variety of visiting speakers. Through the kindness of Professor Edgar E. Robinson, I was invited to join a dinner club in San Francisco which enabled me to meet several professors of the University of California. As chaplain, I was drawn closely to people in their joys and sorrows. For example, when the only child of Clare Boothe Luce was killed near Palo Alto, in an automobile accident, I came to feel very close to both Henry Luce and to his distinguished wife. Though the duties at Stanford were demanding, the rewards were commensurate.

9
Earlham College

In the summer of 1945 we made a major decision. The decision was to leave Stanford University in order to join a small college somewhere. Since Stanford was, and is, a center of cultural and academic magnificence, the very idea of leaving it seemed strange. Later, in an essay published in the *Reader's Digest*, I tried to explain the odd decision, the essay being called, "Why I Chose a Small College." The essence of my thinking centered upon the question where academic excellence is likely to be either found or produced. I saw vividly that bigness, rather than being an inevitable asset, may be a liability. I knew, of course, that mere smallness could not assure greatness, but I also knew that what I sought would be more likely to appear under some conditions than others. I knew, above all, that I wanted to invest my life in a place in which the human contacts could be supremely personal.

Among other things, I sought a situation in which spiritual commitment could be combined creatively with high academic standards. I realized, after nine years of involvement in a great university, that, so far as spiritual commitment is concerned, the great university is not a manageable unit. What is gained in one part of the undertaking is almost certain to be lost in another. Much later, in the late sixties of our century, there came a sorrowful confirmation of my fears about bigness when the worst excesses of violence appeared in enormous institutions, including those in Berkeley, New York, and Cambridge.

Having made the general decision, the particular choice was a relatively easy one. With several opportunities available, I chose Earlham College, Richmond, Indiana. There were several convincing reasons for this choice. One reason was the character of the existing faculty, which included individuals whom I admired, especially for their dedication. When I joined the Earlham faculty in August 1946, the highest salary received by any professor was $2,800 a year. Several of these persons had been offered larger stipends in other and more affluent institutions, but had remained at Earlham on a basis of conviction. They were in full agreement with the idea that financial reward is, of itself, never an adequate reason for change of occupation. In my own case I joined Earlham at a salary exactly half of what I could have received elsewhere.

Between the departure from California and settlement at Richmond I taught the winter quarter at Wabash College and later went to Europe under the care of the Friends Ambulance Unit. The latter step was motivated by my desire to be among Germans who were pulling out of the disaster of the war. Fortunately, I made the acquaintance of Landrum Bolling on the way.

As we began the autumn semester at Earlham in September 1946, there was a pervading sense of intellectual excitement. With the war over, nearly all of the men and women students knew why they had come to college. The fact that many had endured hardships during war years gave an added character to the entire academic undertaking. In all of my years of teaching I have never, at any other time, known so many students who were receptive to learning.

My new course called General Philosophy, based deliberately upon the strategy recommended by Alfred North Whitehead, involved 106 students. I tried not only to make each lecture an exciting occasion, but also to arrange a personal contact with every member of the class. This was made possible by using the hour immediately following each lecture to take six or seven selected students to the coffee shop for further discussion. Each student wrote an essay each week. In order to secure an outside view, I invited a Yale philosopher to visit Earlham, at the end of the semester, as the examiner. I knew, of course, that this scholar was testing me as well as my students because we were, in fact, on the same side of the table.

My appointment as professor of philosophy lasted twenty years, 1946-1966, with a brief interlude for public service in Washington, with the United States Information Agency. Even during the Washington period I returned to the Earlham campus once each month in order to keep the connection intact.

When retirement came in June 1966, President Landrum Bolling graciously proposed that I be designated Professor-at-Large. The purpose of this language was to make clear that, though I was liberated from formal teaching, I could always think of myself as a member of the Earlham faculty, no matter where my travels might take me. Soon we went to London for eight months, and on around the world in an easterly direction. One of our reasons for absence was that I wanted to make sure that I did not, by my presence, interfere in any way with my successor in the philosophy department, Robert Horn.

My relation to the college, since retirement, has been a pleasant one, partly because I have experienced the friendly support of Dr. Bolling's successor, President Franklin Wallin. Though free to attend the faculty meetings, I have never done so. It came as a happy surprise when Earlham, on June 7, 1981, awarded me an honorary doctorate.

The most vivid evidence of our continued involvement in the life of Earlham is that of the location of our home, Virginia Cottage, and of Teague Library, which is my study for as long as I am able to use it. These two buildings, both constructed in conscious conformity to Williamsburg style, have stunning views of the front campus, which is reminiscent of the park at Earlham Hall, England. Here we can welcome students and others as long as our strength holds. We hope we can continue to live in this pleasant situation for many added years.

10
Mount Holyoke College

When I completed my duties at Earlham College in June 1966, it appeared that my teaching, in any structured sense, was over; but it turned out that, in this, I was wrong. Three years later I accepted the welcome invitation to join the faculty of Mount Holyoke College on a temporary basis, and this led to my teaching full time for the semester beginning February 1, 1970. The prospect of serving again in our beloved New England was an attractive one which turned out to be highly rewarding. The experience rounded out my career, in that I had already taught in coeducational institutions, and also in Haverford, then limited to men. Finally I was privileged to serve in an excellent institution specializing in the education of women.

Though I have not been in physical touch with Mount Holyoke since June 1970, I have maintained my interest and am glad to go on record to the effect that I think the college trustees were wise when they decided to counter the coeducational trend. This is not because I think education for women is better education, but rather that the historic pattern is one option which I think ought to be provided *somewhere*. If excellence is to be achieved and maintained, the tendency to blind conformity in higher education is something to be opposed.

Upon our arrival at the attractive village of South Hadley, in the winter of 1970, we settled at once into an apartment easily accessible by foot to the campus. I made it a point to be in the office assigned to me by eight every morning, partly to be available to students who needed to discuss their academic work. The office was located in the building attached to the college library, thus providing me with easy access to the book stacks. Each morning, as I walked, often through deep snow, I passed through the Mary Lyon Gate with a sense of reverence. I was keenly aware that I was observing the scene where serious higher education for women had really begun, so far as America is concerned. I thanked God for Mary Lyon because she was truly a pioneer.

We quickly made new friendships at South Hadley and we have been glad for their endurance. This is particularly true of our friendship with Professor and Mrs. Robert Berkey. I attended all faculty meetings and participated in their discussions. This was important because the climax of student unrest had come at this time. Indeed, we lived through the student strike, in which we tried to play a reconciling role. With the strong support of the president of the college, I arranged a special gathering in the college chapel, on the thesis that, in a critical situation, it is better to pray than to argue or to fight. Fortunately, with the chapel building filled to the very walls, a new spirit seemed to emerge. Before we left for the summer the strike was abandoned and a friendly atmosphere was restored.

With our deep love of New England, we welcomed the opportunity of sharing the life outside the college. We drove several times to Springfield and once to Cambridge, where I was able make connections which helped in the preparation of my book *Abraham Lincoln: Theologian of American Anguish*. At Harvard Square, from which I had been absent for a long time, I was saddened by the evidence of student destruction of property. It will be hard for our descendants to believe how violent the mood of 1970 really was, but I remember because I lived through it.

One of the sources of satisfaction to me in the Mount Holyoke semester arose from the formation of a faculty luncheon group which met weekly for the sharing of ideas over a simple meal. The formation of the group was similar to that of the many other groups which I have had the privilege to nurture in a variety of institutions. I discovered, by conversations, that though many of my new colleagues were personally committed Christians, they had no practical way in which to share their faith with one another. One might suppose that such sharing would be part of normal college or church experience, but I soon realized that such is not the case. One happy surprise was the participation of a totally blind man whom I had known as a young student when I was acting dean of the chapel at Harvard in the summer of 1935. To find this man, after thirty-five years, as both a respected professor and a deeply committed Christian was satisfying, indeed. My conscious purpose, with my new colleagues, was to build a fire and to leave it burning. To meet some of them in England later was a special satisfaction. We met the Berkeys at the University of Cambridge and Professor Norma Adams in London.

Another opportunity, provided by temporary residence at South Hadley, was that of trying to strengthen local churches in the general vicinity. Free from duties on weekends, we sometimes attended the Sunday chapel service at the college, but more often I spoke in the small churches when invited to do so. I came to see freedom to give my services as I chose as an especially fortunate kind of liberation.

My chief literary work during that spring of 1970 was devoted to the planning of a book which became *The Future of the Christian*. The chapters were begun at South Hadley and completed in Indiana after our residence in New England was ended. The exciting idea, on which I labored, was that of the miracle of survival, so far as the Christian faith is concerned. As I heard people confidently announcing the end of the Christian movement, I was convinced that they were wrong. The evidence that they were wrong, I concluded, was not dogma, but *experience*. I was amazed, as I meditated on the fact that the faith has survived opposition in various periods of human history. I concluded accordingly that we are still living in the early days of the faith.

11
Stout Meetinghouse

The construction of the Stout Meetinghouse on the Earlham campus, in 1951-52, gave me more satisfaction than most events in my long life. As soon as I began my Earlham residence, in the late summer of 1946, I began to discuss with President Thomas E. Jones and others the prospect of a building devoted to the encouragement of the spiritual life. This was because the lack of such a center was conspicuous. I knew that, in 1847, on the death of Joseph John Gurney, of Earlham Hall, England, a sum of money had been given from the Gurney estate, with the construction of a meetinghouse in mind; but I also knew that the severe financial strain of starting a new institution had caused the money to be diverted to other uses. In the ensuing century the project had been mentioned often, but by 1946 nothing concrete had been done. What I soon learned was that the interest was intense and that the building we had in mind might become one concrete mark of the new vitality that was evident.

Right away small gifts of money were subscribed for the project, but, in the midst of many other duties, no organized effort was launched. However, I told President Jones that I gladly accepted the meeting-house project as my part of the labor of strengthening the entire college program. We did not have a precise location in mind, and we had only a few thousand dollars; but we had a potent dream, and that sufficed for the moment. It was already obvious that the venture was not likely to be accomplished without at least one big gift, but of the source of such a gift we had no distinct idea.

From the start we recognized the fact that the recognition of Earlham's English roots would be of advantage in our ambitious undertaking. If we could have some real connection with the Gurneys of Earlham, we thought, the incentive would be heightened. It was general knowledge that Joseph John Gurney, on his remarkable American journey in 1837, had traveled as far west as Richmond, Indiana, and had said that there ought to be a college on what was then the American frontier. The employment of the name of the famous Gurney estate near Norwich, in East Anglia, was a natural development when the new institution needed a name. The word "Earlham" carried with it valuable overtones, in that the Norwich estate had been the scene of many important social and spiritual developments. In the early years of the nineteenth century many gatherings devoted to the antislavery movement were held in the spacious home of the Gurneys, and much of Elizabeth Gurney Fry's pioneer work in prison reform was stimulated there. By reading Percy Lubbock's fascinating book *Earlham* and dipping into the journal of various Gurneys, I had some idea of how great the vitality in one place could be. During my residence at Birmingham, England, in the winter of 1939, as Fellow of Woodbrooke, I had already seen at first hand a few of the Gurney literary treasures. And then there came a development I could not have foreseen.

In June 1948 the earthly life of Rufus Jones ended, at the age of eighty-five. As soon as my college duties were completed, I went at once to the Haverford campus to see whether there was something I could do to lift the inevitable burdens of Elizabeth Cadbury Jones, Professor Jones's widow. Very quickly she said she needed help, especially in correspondence, since the numerous letters were far beyond the ability of one person to handle.

Accepting the responsibility, I soon saw a letter from Doris Eddington, of Norwich, England, referring to the recent death of her own husband, Arthur Eddington, who asked her, on his deathbed, to approach Rufus Jones on a subject very near to his heart. This subject was the old Wymondham meetinghouse, which was then about to be dismantled and turned into a residence. This meetinghouse, situated about twenty miles west of Earlham Hall, long the home of the Gurneys, was often attended by the Gurney young people, particularly Elizabeth, who became famous as Elizabeth Fry, and her brothers, Joseph, John, and Samuel. It seemed a shame, Arthur Eddington thought, to allow the old benches, tiles, and beams to be destroyed. He wondered whether some American college might be able to use these, if they were donated by their owners, Norwich Friends.

It did not take me long to answer Mrs. Eddington, saying that we were planning to build a meetinghouse on the Earlham campus and that, in my judgment, the Wymondham relics would be much appreciated as parts of the new building. I realized that this would give the new building some touch of antiquity and also forge a genuine link between Earlham in America and Earlham in England. In my letter to Doris Eddington, I explained that I could make a visit to England that summer and spend some time with Norwich Friends.

The ship passage to England was arranged, and soon I was able to go by train from London to Norwich. I could hardly wait to see the furnishings, which included oak beams more than two hundred years old. Though the gift was made in 1948, the problems connected with export license and packing prevented actual delivery in Richmond, Indiana, for more than two years. Accordingly, the meetinghouse furnishings were still intact in the summer of 1950 when I visited Norwich with my family.

The committee in charge of the building of the Stout Meetinghouse at Earlham soon decided to put the old facing benches in a separate meditation room, to be called the "Quiet Room"; and there they are to this day, valued by many who make use of them, especially in small groups. The committee also decided to put the finest of the oak beams in the middle room and to call this the "Wymondham Room." A beam today surmounts the fireplace in this room and is perfectly preserved, in spite of its age. It was also decided to use the Wymondham tiles to make hearths for the three fireplaces of the building. The balustrade at the east end of the meetinghouse library is made of wood which came from the Wymondham meetinghouse.

Once we had these assets in place, we realized that the Wymondham Room could be made far more valuable by adding paintings of the persons involved. We were fortunate in receiving splendid gifts of the portraits of both Elizabeth Fry and Joseph John Gurney from the Gurney family of Norwich. It is highly appropriate that Joseph John

Gurney, the man who was really the spiritual founder of Earlham College, should be represented in this fashion. The Wymondham Room also includes a portrait of Arthur Eddington, who had the first idea of a transfer of furnishings from England to America.

With the gifts from England secure, we were ready for the main effort of raising the funds and planning both the character and location of the desired building. By a fortunate series of events it became clear that the Stout family, centered at Paoli, Indiana, provided the best hope for the necessary major gift. Accordingly I traveled, a year after my first Norwich trip, to visit Mr. and Mrs. Charles Stout, of Memphis, Tennessee. Though all of the children of John Stout were interested, Charles was the one who was in a position to make a really substantial gift. I took the night train from Cincinnati to Memphis, spent the entire day with the Stouts and returned by train the following night. To my immense relief Charles Stout whispered to me as I entered the train in the Memphis station that the funds necessary for the construction of a meetinghouse on the Earlham campus would be forthcoming.

With the money assured, the next task was design. Our committee on plans took its work seriously, part of its work being that of visits to exciting buildings which appeared to be functional and aesthetic. We knew at once that we wanted to retain the simplicity of early American style, but we also knew that we ought to provide modern facilities such as a library and a day nursery. As we looked at beautiful older buildings, particularly the meetinghouses of Abington, Pennsylvania, and Sandy Spring, Maryland, we studied very carefully the proportions. Already we recognized that whatever beauty might be achieved was likely to come from pleasing proportions rather than from any decorations. We have been happy about the result.

Location was also important. It was decreed that the new building should be close enough to others to ensure ease of access, but enough removed to provide a sense of peace. This combination was achieved by using space at the southwest corner of the main campus, among noble trees, very few of which it was necessary to remove.

Very early it was decided that, so far as possible, the new building should be produced by voluntary labor. The result was that at least five hundred persons, including students, professors, and townspeople gave their labor, wholly without remuneration. To make sure that this unusual action would not cause labor trouble we sought and won the assent of the chief labor union of Richmond. Some employed carpenters, electricians, and masons were, of course, needed to provide continuity, and it was especially important to have some skilled foreman, to guide those of us who were amateurs. We were fortunate to be able to employ Earl Prignitz, who combined professional skills with undoubted dedication. The building process went forward for over a year, without undue hurry, and was completed in the spring of 1952. Even the comfortable benches, most of which are now located in the large meeting room, were actually produced within the walls of the new meetinghouse. They were made of native poplar.

As it now stands, the handsome building called Stout Meetinghouse contains five major sections. The first, to the east, graced by a long early American porch, has clear glass windows and is filled with the handmade benches which are usually arranged in a hollow square, to provide a maximum sense of being members one of another. The benches are free from any floor fastening, thus providing for different arrangements when desired. The balcony to the west is designed for overflow at the end of the library. Without crowding, the room seats four hundred people.

The room to the west of the main lobby is called the Wymondham Room because of materials from the old building in East Anglia. The walls are adorned by paintings and engravings already mentioned. Over the fireplace, with its oak beam more than two centuries old, is a well-used ox yoke, which was donated by the late H. V. Scott, a Fort Wayne physician who long served as chairman of Yokefellows International. Doctor Scott gave the handsome yoke in 1952, at the time of dedication of the building. It is a constant reminder of Christ's clearest call to commitment, "Take my yoke upon you, and learn of me" (Matt. 11:29, King James Version).

The dominant feature of the Wymondham Room is the great cherry table, surrounded by cherry armchairs. The table has provided a setting for countless seminars in its thirty years of use, and has moved many by its beauty. The solid cherry wood of the oval table was provided by a gift from the late Rose Dougan, of Richmond. One day in 1949 Miss Dougan, while driving in her car, saw workmen cutting an immense cherry tree. Recognizing its value, she stopped and bought the tree on the spot. She then arranged to have the wood sawn into planks, each at least sixteen feet long, and had them stored in the basement of her home. She then gave this treasure to Earlham. The planks were stored for a year and then were kiln-dried, to avoid all danger of warping. The task of finding a cabinet worker able and willing to turn the planks into a table was not an easy one, but finally a workman was found who built the table in a room behind his house in Richmond. His own modest life was ennobled by the undertaking, partly because he admired the parabolic shape of the top and the unusual legs which he constructed by hand. It was especially fortunate that the college was able to employ the late Wilford Nuss of Centerville, Indiana, to achieve the brilliant finish which endures almost perfectly to the present time. Partly because of the beauty of the great table, it has been preserved with care by its many users.

The Quiet Room, on the northwest corner, is provided with a separate entrance to accommodate those who wish to make use of it without going through the rest of the building. It is designed for both individual prayer and small gatherings. It has even been the scene of small weddings. The striking feature of the Quiet Room is the presence of the Wymondham benches which, for many decades, provided seating for those deemed most likely to speak in the meetings. One engraving on the wall depicts a woman speaking in a similar setting. A conscious decision was made to leave the benches exactly as they were when they crossed the Atlantic in 1951. Accordingly they have not been refinished. The original drawing for the painting over the fireplace was discovered in London and hangs on the wall.

A fourth section of the Stout Meetinghouse is the library, occupying the upstairs room. It is supplied with browsing books of good quality, the purchase of these being made possible by a gift from the late Alvin T. Coate of Indianapolis. The library space is frequently used for committee meetings and sometimes for classes. The most striking feature of the library is that of the valuable Spence etchings depicting scenes mentioned in the *Journal* of George Fox and donated by the late Sturge sisters of Birmingham, England. The fifth section of the meetinghouse is the scene of the Pauline Trueblood Nursery, which provides day care for young children whose mothers share in a cooperative effort.

Index

Eisenhower, Dwight D., 47, 48, 49
Eisenhower, Milton, 48
Eliot, T. S., 75, 83
Elson, Edward, 24
Emerson Hall, 101
Emerson, Ralph Waldo, 115
Erteszek, Jan and Olga, 24
Eves, Anna, 108
Exman, Eugene, 39, 58

Faunce, W. H. P., 110, 111
Fisher, Agnes, 82
Fisher, Melita, 24
Fisk University, 62, 64
Fosdick, Harry Emerson, 38, 39, 40, 54
Fox, George, 83, 140
Friend, The, 56, 57, 58, 123, 126
Friends Ambulance Unit, 44, 129
Friends School, Baltimore, 119
Friends University, 24
Friends World Conference, 56
Fry, Elizabeth, 83, 135, 136

Gallahue, Dorothy, 53
Gallahue, Edward, 53, 54, 55
Gettysburg, 48, 76
Gettysburg College, 48
Gifford Lectures, 52, 59
Godwin, Johnnie, 7
Gray, Thomas, 76
Guilford College, 111, 116, 117, 118
Gummere, Amelia, 23, 123
Gurney, Joseph John, 134, 136

Hamilton, Edith, 41, 42, 43
Haverford College, 30, 56, 91, 111, 122, 123, 124, 125, 131
Harper & Row, 52, 58
Hay, John, 79
Harvard Square, 12, 132
Harvard University, 35, 57, 74, 110, 111, 113, 114, 115
Hegel, 113, 123
Hocking, William Ernest 115

Homewood Meeting House, 120
Hoover, Herbert C., 33, 34, 69, 70, 126
Hoover, Herbert Jr., 33
Hoover, Lou Henry, 33, 126
Hoover, Mrs. Tad, 33
Horace, 23
Horn, Robert, 130

Iona, 76, 85, 86
Iowa State University, 24

John Hay Library, 101
Johns Hopkins University, 48, 119, 120, 121, 123
Johnson, Samuel, 11, 12, 13, 16, 19, 21, 23, 38, 76, 82
Jones, Elizabeth, 30, 32, 123, 135
Jones, Mary Hoxie, 30
Jones, Rufus M., 30, 31, 32, 38, 39, 56, 122, 123, 135
Jones, Thomas E., 44, 62, 63, 64, 134
Jordan, Mrs. David Starr, 23
Justinian, 74

Kant, Immanuel, 123
Kelly, Thomas R., 56, 57, 58
Kempis, Thomas á., 116
Kirk, Jack, 7
Kobayashi, Tetsuo and Emily, 24

Lake Mohonk, 90, 91
Lake Paupac, 87, 88
Lawrence, T. E., 69
Lee, Ann, 93
Lilly, Eli, 44, 45, 46, 64, 93, 94
Lilly Endowment, 45, 64
Lilly Library, 45
Lincoln, Abraham, 47, 49, 50, 51
Lincoln Memorial, 76
Livingstone, David, 75
London, 82, 83, 84
London Yearly Meeting, 85
Lowell House, 114
Lowell Lectures, 35

Lovejoy, Arthur O., 103, 119, 120, 121
Lubbock, Percy, 135
Luce, Clare Boothe, 127
Luce, Henry, 127
Lyon, Mary, 131, 132

MacLeod, George, 85, 86, 95, 96
Marathon, 76
McGuffey, William H., 80, 81
Meier, Rodger, 24
Meyerson, Emile, 57
Mill, John Stuart, 17
Milton, John, 22, 81
Moore, George Foot, 115
Moses Brown School, 30
Mott, John R., 27, 28, 29
Mount Holyoke College, 30, 111, 131, 132, 133
Muggeridge, Malcolm, 21
Murray, Augustus T., 23
Murray, Sir Gilbert, 74

National Presbyterian Church, 47, 48
Negro College Fund, 62
Neill, Bishop Stephen, 21
New Harmony, 95, 96
Newby, James, 24
Niebuhr, Reinhold, 50, 51, 52
North Methodist Church, 53, 54
Nuss, Wilford, 139

Orr, Dr. William, 24
Owen, Mrs. Kenneth, 95
Owen, Robert, 95, 96
Oxford University, 113

Pascal, Blaise, 23, 116
Paupac Lodge, 89
Peale, Norman Vincent, 68
Penn, William, 22, 83
Perry, Bliss, 115
Personalism, 20
Philadelphia Yearly Meeting, 51
Pickett, Clarence E., 23

Pitman, Robert, 22
Plato, 10, 11, 14, 15, 18, 23, 24, 37, 41, 42, 101
Pleasant Hill, 94
Pocono Mountains, 87, 89
Prignitz, Earl, 138
Promised Land, 87
Purdy, Alexander C., 23, 110

Quiller-Couch, Sir Arthur, 102

Radhakrishnan, 21
Raines, Richard, 54, 55
Rapp, George, 95, 96
Reader's Digest, 128
Rhodes, Cecil, 75
River Brethren, 47
Riverside Church, 38, 40
Robinson, Edgar E., 127
Rockefeller, John D., Jr., 38, 63, 110
Rogers, Ada, 103
Roth, Hans, 24
Royce, Josiah, 119
Russell, Elbert, 23

Schliemann, H., 46
Schreiner, Olive, 75
Schweitzer, Albert, 121
Scott, H. V., 138
Shakertown, 93, 94
Simpson College, 100, 105
Smiley, Albert K., 90, 92
Smiley, Alfred, 90
Smiley Family, 91
Socrates, 10, 17, 22, 23, 36
South Hadley, 131, 133
Sperry, Willard L., 110, 113, 114, 115, 116
St. Andrews University, 59
St. Bartholomew's Church, 68
St. Paul's Cathedral, 83
Stanford Memorial Church, 125
Stanford University, 24, 35, 50, 62, 101, 111, 114, 125, 126, 127
Steere, Douglas, 58, 122